Need A Chakra Reset Button?

A 126 Day Chakra

Alignment.

D. Krystal Starr

Copyright © 2011 D Krystal Adams All rights reserved.

ISBN-13: 978-0615525518

PREFACE

Swami Kriyananda

This is a most intriguing book! I would very much like to know how many people are helped by it, and how deeply. The subject itself is fascinating: the spinal centers in our bodies; how they affect us; the present and potential ways they affect our consciousness.

Paramhansa Yogananda, in his world-known book Autobiography of a Yogi, states that thoughts are universally, not inidividually, rooted. This means that our brains do not produce the ideas that come out of them: they merely express concepts that belong to whatever level of consciousness we are living at, at the time. Any change in our level of consciousness alters instantly our very view of reality.

The levels of reality we perceive depend entirely on where, in the spine, our energy and consciousness are centered. The chakras, viewed outwardly, simply channel energy to different regions of the body: the heart, the stomach, the sex organs, the legs, etc. Viewed inwardly, however—that is to say, when that same energy is withdrawn to the spine and directed upward toward the brain—the chakras become portals that open onto ever-increasing enlightenment. The spinal chakras, therefore, are of central importance to the science of yoga.

I pray that this book will help many people better to know their own inner selves.

Chapter 1 - Page 15

16: ROOT Opening day: Work with all chakras.

17: Section 1: Opening with Air

Visualize - Prayer - Crystal Healing - Ritual

22: Section 2: Water Cleanses

Visualize - Prayer - Crystal Healing - Ritual

27: Section 3: Fire Energizes

Visualize - Prayer - Crystal Healing - Ritual

33: Section 4: Earth Protects and Strengthens

Visualize - Prayer - Crystal Healing - Ritual

39: Root Closing day: Work with all chakras.

Chapter 2 - Page 40

41: NAVEL Opening day: work with all chakras.

41: Section 1: Opening with Air

Visualize - Prayer - Crystal Healing - Ritual

47: Section 2: Water Cleanses

Visualize - Prayer - Crystal Healing - Ritual

53: Section 3: Fire Energizes

Visualize - Prayer - Crystal Healing - Ritual

59: Section 4: Earth Protects and Strengthens

Visualize - Prayer - Crystal Healing - Ritual

65: Navel Closing day: Work with all chakras.

Chapter 3 - Page 66

67: Solar Plexus Opening day: work with all chakras.

68: Section 1: Opening with Air

Visualize - Prayer - Crystal Healing - Ritual

74: Section 2: Water Cleanses

Visualize - Prayer - Crystal Healing - Ritual

80: Section 3: Fire Energizes

Visualize - Prayer - Crystal Healing - Ritual

86: Section 4: Earth Protects and Strengthens

Visualize - Prayer - Crystal Healing - Ritual

91: Solar Plexus Closing day: Work with all chakras.

Chapter 4 - Page 92

93: Heart Opening day: work with all chakras.

93: Section 1: Opening with Air

Visualize - Prayer - Crystal Healing - Ritual

98: Section 2: Water Cleanses

Visualize - Prayer - Crystal Healing - Ritual

105: Section 3: Fire Energizes

Visualize - Prayer - Crystal Healing - Ritual

111: Section 4: Earth Protects and Strengthens

Visualize - Prayer - Crystal Healing - Ritual

117: Heart Closing day: Work with all chakras.

Chapter 5 - Page 118

119: Throat Opening day: work with all chakras.

119: Section 1: Opening with Air

Visualize - Prayer - Crystal Healing - Ritual

125: Section 2: Water Cleanses

Visualize Prayer Crystal Healing Ritual

130: Section 3: Fire Energizes

Visualize - Prayer - Crystal Healing - Ritual

136: Section 4: Earth Protects and Strengthens

Visualize - Prayer - Crystal Healing - Ritual

140: Throat Closing day: Work with all chakras.

Chapter 6 - Page 141

142: 3rd eye Opening day: work with all chakras.

143: Section 1: Opening with Air

Visualize - Prayer - Crystal Healing - Ritual

148: Section 2: Water Cleanses

Visualize - Prayer - Crystal Healing - Ritual

154: Section 3: Fire Energizes

Visualize - Prayer - Crystal Healing - Ritual

159: Section 4: Earth Protects and Strengthens

Visualize - Prayer - Crystal Healing - Ritual

165: 3rd Eye Closing day: Work with all chakras.

Chapter 7 - page 166

167: Crown Opening day: work with all chakras.

168: Section 1: Opening with Air

Visualize - Prayer - Crystal Healing - Ritual

172: Section 2: Water Cleanses

Visualize - Prayer - Crystal Healing - Ritual

177: Section 3: Fire Energizes

Visualize - Prayer - Crystal Healing - Ritual

182: Section 4: Earth Protects and Strengthens

Visualize - Prayer - Crystal Healing - Ritual

187: Crown Closing day: Work with all chakras.

Introduction

Ever wish there was a magical Chakra Reset button? Unfortunately, there isn't one. This process will take you 126 days. The good news is that this guide is for those who need to completely shift their lives around!

The chakras hold energy from all the lives you've ever lived. Thus, when the chakras are not in harmonious alignment it can have a *drastic* effect on your life and your physical body. This 126-day process is not for those who are looking for a light chakra boost. This is for those of you who need an intense healing.

We will work on the seven Chakras for 18 days each. We will open them with Air, cleanse them with Water, energize them with Fire, and strengthen them with Earth – one by one.

By harmonizing the four elements in each of the seven chakras, you will enable the elements to begin working *together*, free of negativity and disharmony! With each element, you will perform four steps (one per day). Then you will move on to the next element and repeat the four steps until all of the elements are aligned and harmonized.

At that point, you can move on to the next chakra.

It doesn't matter if a chakra is over-active, under-active, or completely closed. Regardless, it is necessary to work on all of the chakras, even if you only want to heal just one chakra.

Let's get started!

Special Thanks

I want to thank God first and foremost, for the ability to reach out and help, and for all the wonderful things he has given me in this lifetime!

I also want to thank Swami Kriyananda for the guidance he has given me. He taught me what it really means to heal and help a person from the bottom of your heart, and he was my

inspiration for writing this book.

He has accomplished so much throughout his

lifetime.

Ananda (the spiritual community he has built)

Is full of the most amazing people I have ever

met. His soul is unlike any other I have seen.

He is untouched by the energy of the physical

world, even though he is still in his physical body. His spirit is on such a high level of vibration that he is a part of the spiritual world more than he is of the physical world. This is something we all aspire to be! He has been such an amazing guide in this lifetime, and I feel as though he has been a guide in all his lifetimes, one way or another.

It has certainly been an honor to receive that guidance. Thank you!

I want to thank my mother and grandmother for teaching me so much.

John for being supportive in everything I do.

My spiritual sister Narayani for always caring and praying for me, and Asha Praver for her inspiration.

Using The Four Elements.

Not only are we going to work on each chakra, but we are going to use each of the four elements (Earth, Air, Fire and water) one at a time with each chakra before moving forward to the next one. We are going to use the Air element to open, The Water element to cleanse, The Fire element to energize, and the Earth element to ground and strengthen your spirit. There are certain crystals you will need to use when your working with certain elements. You can choose one stone or crystal for each element out of the following list...

Air: Aventurine, Mottled Jasper, Mica, Pumice

Water: Blue Lace Agate, Amethyst, Aquamarine, Azurite, Blue and Pink Calcite, Chrysocolla,

Fire: Banded, Black, Brown, Red Agate, Amber, Apache Tear, Bloodstone, Carnelian, Citrine,

Earth: Green Agate, Green Calcite, Cat's-eye, Chrysoprase, Coal, Emerald, Brown and Green

Tips and Suggestions

1. It's always good to take five minutes before you begin a step, to relax and allow the chakra to open.

2. You may have another person help you with the Crystal Healing steps, if you find that it makes it easier for you.

3. If you are unable to put your hands in one of the Mudras, then just keep your hands open and palms upward.

4. Try wearing the color of the chakra you are working on – or the color white. (We will describe the colors later.)

Chapter One: ROOT

Sanskrit Name: Muladhara

Chant: Lam

Location: Tailbone

Stones: Smoky Quartz, Hematite, Black Tourmaline, Onyx

Scent: Sandalwood, Corn, Rosemary, Heritage Rose

Color: Red

Properties when healed: Survival, Vitality, Reality, Grounding, Security, Support, Stability, Individuality, Courage,

Properties when over-active: Impulsiveness, Greed, Resistance to Change

Properties when under-active: Fear, Feeling Unwelcome, Nervousness

Associated body parts: Spine (Chi, Life Force) Legs, Feet, Bones, Teeth, Large Intestine, Prostate, Bladder, Blood, Circulation, Tailbone

Information stored inside root chakra: Familial Beliefs, Superstitions, Loyalty, Instincts, Physical Pleasure or Pain, Touch

Opening Day of the Root - Day 1

1. As you inhale, speak the first part of this phrase. 2. As you exhale, speak the second part of this phrase. 3. Repeat each of the twelve incantations ten times.

(Inhale) "My energy" – (Exhale) "is free of blockages."

(Inhale) "My root chakra" – (Exhale) "is centered."

(Inhale) "My Navel Chakra juices" – (Exhale) "are Passionate."

(Inhale) "My solar plexus" – (Exhale)

"feels confident."

(Inhale) "My heart" – (Exhale) "Gives and receives love."

(Inhale) "My throat" – (Exhale) "speaks the truth."

(Inhale) "My third eye" – (Exhale) "Sees past the physical world."

(Inhale) "My Crown Chakra" – "Exhale is full of wisdom."

(Inhale) "My chakras" – (Exhale) "are spinning in alignment."

Section: 1 - Root - Element: Opening with Air – Step: Visual - Day 2

To bring in the air element, you will do the visual next to a window or outside in the fresh air. Put both hands in Root Mudra Position. This will allow you to send energy into the Root Chakra. Keep the Root stone in your right hand and the Air Stone in the left.

Lay on your stomach on the floor or ground. Visualize a Red Ball of Light hovering over you. There is a tube connecting you to the ball of red light going straight into your tail bone. As you breathe in you are taking in the energy from the ball of light above you, into the tube and straight into your chakra. Breath in and hold it in for 5 seconds and let your root chakra absorb it. Then exhale and as you breathe out you send it into the ground. It is centering and grounding you. Keep doing this until you have inhaled a total of 10 times – or longer if you feel the need.

Section: 1 - Root – Element: Opening with Air – Step: Prayer - Day 3

Today we will do a prayer to open the Root Chakra.

You do not need any stones or tools. You will rely only on your connection to God.

I pray for the air to blow open the door to my root chakra.

Blow away any obstacles that keep me from feeling centered and grounded. Once this door is open, I will do everything in my power to cleanse, energize, and protect it!

I pray for a burst of wind to shoot straight up

through barriers that have been put up around my root chakra.
No more will I feel unsteady or confused about where I belong.
I will never feel Fear and Insecurity like this again.
I will see my destiny and feel safe and secure in my home.
I pray to God to feel and hear the rush of the wind blowing through my open root chakra! – so that I can be Grounded, and Centered, and have the strength to keep moving forward on the path that God has laid out for me. Amen

Section: 1 - Root – Element: Opening with Air – – Step: Crystal Healing - Day 4

Lie on your stomach, somewhere where you can feel a breeze, and place the Root Stone on your spine. Put both hands opened, palms facing upward with the Air Stone in the opposite hand of your writing hand. Remain like this for 5 minutes while the crystals open this chakra.

Then use your writing hand to move the Root Stone as far up your spine as you can reach, and all the way back down.

Do this 50 times.

Then leave the crystal near the base of your spine, or in the small of your back, and rest your hand back down on the floor, palm up, for a few minutes. When you are ready, take the crystal and rub it in a circle at the base of your spine. Make 50 circles.

Then sit up and take the Root Stone in your writing hand. Put both hands in the Root Mudra Position. Both hands should now be in the Root Mudra Position, with the Root Stone in your writing hand and the Air Stone in the other hand. Remain like this for at least 10 minutes – longer if needed.

Section: 1 - Root – Element: Opening with Air – Step: Ritual - Day 5

Sit somewhere outside, away from your home. A park or beach would do well. Place a ring of rock salt around you. Bring seven bits of paper (or a large piece of paper that you can cut into seven pieces), as well as a pen, a Root Stone, and a, Air Stone. Place the Air Stone on the ring of salt directly in front of you, and keep the Root Stone in your right hand. Sit with your hands in the Root Mudra Position while your root chakra opens.

Next, write the following seven lines, one line on each piece of paper. (Keep the stone in either hand that feels comfortable while you copy the lines.) Place the first written line underneath the Air Stone on the salt ring, and place the other lines following in a clockwise direction around the ring. (It's okay if the air blows the paper away after you place it around the circle.)

1. *"May the Air burst through"*: This line will go under the Air Stone in front of you.
2. *"and open my Root Chakra"* Place this

line next to the first one in a clockwise direction.

3. *"So I can Cleanse with the water element"* Keep placing the lines around in a circle clockwise...

4. *"Energize with the fire element"*

5. *"And protect it with the earth element."*

6. *"By using the four elements"*

7. *"I will be completely aligned."*

You may sit with your hands in the Root Mudra Position again for 5 to 10 minutes. Leave everything but the stones where they are, then leave to do not look back.

Section: 2 - Root – Element: Cleansing

with Water – – Step: Visual - Day 6

To bring in the water element, you will do the visual in a tub, ocean, pool, lake, or anyplace that allows you to be half-submerged in water. Put your hands in the Root Mudra position. Keep the Root Stone in your right hand, and the Water Stone in the left.

Sit down in the water and close your eyes. Visualize that the water you are submerged in is a Red Healing Liquid for your spirit. When you are able to fully see the bright liquid in your mind's eye, take a breath.

Every time you breathe in, you are soaking up the liquid into your Root Chakra. Hold it in for 5 seconds and let the root chakra soak in the liquid. As you exhale, repeat "LAM"
And let the liquid drain and rinse out completely. Keep repeating the steps until you have rinsed the chakra at least 10 times. Then allow the liquid to completely fill your body from head to toe.
When you feel ready, leave the water, dry off completely, and sit or stand with your hands in the Root Mudra position. Take your time to visualize the red, liquid you

absorbed inside of your body as it drains out.

After it has drained, you see that it has created a ball of light in your tailbone, and the light is spinning.

Every breath is making the light spin faster. Keep doing this for 10 minutes, or longer if needed.

Section: 2 - Root– Element: Cleansing

with Water – – Step: Prayer - Day 7

I Pray to God for His cleansing holy water to pour though my root chakra. Let it cleanse away all feelings of fear and insecurity. I want to bathe in that cleansing water and see all the blackness that has been obstructing my root chakra for so long clear out once and for all. I pray to feel clean and ready to fill the root chakra with unlimited energizing power. I pray to feel the holy water filling me up inside, and washing me inside and out. I want it to wash away negative energy from my past and leave me feeling STRONGER! So I can be Grounded and Centered, and have the strength to keep moving forward on the path that God has laid out for me. Amen!

Section: 2 - Root
Element: Cleansing with Water
Step: Crystal Healing - Day 8

Lie on your stomach with a bowl of rock salt water close to you, and place the Root Stone on your spine. Put one hand facing upward with a Water Stone in the middle of that palm (the opposite palm of your writing hand). You can let the hand rest

on the floor, as long as it is facing palm up. Keep your writing hand also facing palm up and relaxed.

Remain like this for 5 minutes while the crystals open this chakra.

Then use your writing hand to dip the Root Stone in the water and move it as far up your spine as you can reach, and all the way back down in a wavy line. Allow yourself to feel the drip and wetness of the water on your back. Do this 50 times. Next, leave the crystal near the base of your spine, or in the small of your back, and rest your hand back on the floor again, palm upward, for a few minutes. When you are ready, take the crystal, dip it in the water, and move it in a wavy line across from one hip to the other and back again, crossing the base of the spin in the middle. Do this 50 times. Then sit up and take the Root Stone in your writing hand. Put both hands in the Root Mudra Position. Both hands should now be in the Root Mudra Position, with the Root Stone in your writing hand and the Water Stone in the other hand. Remain like this for at least 10 minutes, longer if needed.

Section: 2 - Root – Element: Cleansing with Water – Step: Ritual - Day 9

You'll need to pick a place with plenty of room, where you would not mind spilling a lot of water. For example, your backyard, or a big round tub or hot tub. Mix one cup of rock salt with a gallon of water. Put the Water Stone and the Root Stone in the gallon of salt water, and let it soak for three hours. Pour salt water into six cups or bowls. (Dispose of whatever water you have remaining.)

Place the six cups around you, surrounding you in a circle. Place the

Water Stone in the circle in front of you. Keep the Root Stone in your right hand.

Repeat the next six lines, one by one. While you are repeating each line, you are going to pour one cup of water over your head (with either hand) for every line you repeat, starting with the cup in front of you and working clockwise. Repeat:

1. "May the Water Element rush through."
Pour the first cup in front of you over your head while you say this. Then take the next cup, and repeat:

2. "And cleanse my Root Chakra."

Keep going around, taking a cup and pouring it over your head as you say each line.

3. "So I can energize with the fire Element."

4. "And protect with the Earth element."

5. "By using the four elements,"

6. "I will be completely aligned."

Remain in the circle for 5 to 10 minutes with your hands in the Root Mudra position and the Root Stone in your right hand.

Section: 3 - Root – Element: Energizing with Fire – – Step: Visual - Day 10

You may do this Visual with your hands in the Root Mudra Position.

Keep the Root Stone in your right hand and the Fire Stone in the left.

Visualize that every breath is igniting a small red flame at the base of your spine. With each breath, the flame grows larger until it is a ball of red fire at the base of your spine. This red fire is energizing you and giving you strength. The red fireball begins to spin, and the energizing feeling increases. In each statement below, I want you to fill in the blank with something in your life that you want to rid yourself of. Whether it is a person, a habit, a house, or a feeling inside of you – ANYTHING! Inhale, hold in for 5 seconds. Let the fire increase in power. Once you feel like the pressure has built up enough, exhale. Every time you exhale, visual the fire striking out a flame in front of you to burn the negative word right up into ashes. Every time you EXHALE, the flame goes out through the front of your body and up toward the spoken words.

(Inhale) "I am Grounded" – (Exhale) "I do not want____"

(Inhale) "I am Centered" – (Exhale) "I do not want____"

(Inhale) I am Healthy" – (Exhale) "I do not want____

(Inhale) "I have unlimited physical energy" – (Exhale) "I do not want____"

Now you feel the fire slowing down until the root chakra it just glowing with a beautiful red light. Now repeat the following:

(Inhale) "My root chakra is energized" (Exhale) "and it always will be."

Section: 3 - Root – Element: Energizing with Fire – Step: Prayer - Day 11

I pray to God to feel the fire from the universe fiercely rushing through my root chakra and energizing me. I pray to feel the heat of the flame raise my vibration to a higher level. I pray for the fire to energize my feeling of centeredness. I pray for the fire to burn away anything keeping me from feeling grounded. I pray for the fire to give me an unlimited amount of physical energy. I pray for fire so I can see which way I am heading and feel safe.

I have nothing to fear, because God has given me the flame of light.
I know who I am because of this light, and I am energized because of the heat of the flame. I allow the heat into my body. I completely and openly allow it to burn away feelings of fear or insecurities. I am at home with the Flame of light, and it will energize my mind, body, and soul.
I pray for this flame so that I can be Grounded and Centered and have the strength to keep moving forward on the path

that God has laid out for me. Amen

Section: 3 - Root– Element: Energizing with Fire — Step: Crystal Healing

Day 12

Leave the Fire Stone next to a lit red or white candle for 3 hours.

Keep the lit candle next to you while you do this Crystal Healing.

Lie on your stomach and place the Root

Stone on your spine. Both hands should be placed palms up. Keep the Fire Stone in the opposite of your writing hand. Remain like this for 5 minutes while the crystals open this chakra.

Then use your writing hand to move the Root Stone in a big triangle on your back – the highest point of the triangle being the farthest up your spine you can reach, and the two bottom corners being your hips. Do this 50 times in a clockwise direction. Then leave the crystal near the base of your spine or in the small of your back, and rest your hand back down on the floor for a few minutes, palm up.

When you are ready, take the crystal and move it in a small triangle just around your tailbone. Do this 50 times.

Then sit up and take the Root Stone in your writing hand.

Put both hands in the Root Mudra position.

Both hands should now be in the Root Mudra position with the Root Stone in your writing hand and Fire Stone in the other hand.

Remain like this for at least 10 minutes, longer if needed.

Section: 3 - Root– Element: Energizing with Fire – Step: Ritual - Day 13

Place five red or white candles around you in a circle. Place the Fire Stone next to the candle in front of you, and keep the Root Stone in your right hand. Let the chakra open for 5 minutes. Hold the Root Stone in whichever hand is comfortable while you do the following steps.

You are going to be writing down five lines – one line on each piece of paper. After you write down the first line, you will burn it in the candle directly in front of you. Then write down the next line and burn it in the next candle in the clockwise direction. (You can keep a bowl or cup of water with you to put the bit of flaming paper for safety after the words have burned.) *1. May the Fire element roar with heat and flame.* Burn this line in the candle in front of you. *2. And energize my Root Chakra.* Burn in the next candle. *3. So I can protect it with the Earth Element.* And so on...

4. By using the four elements.

5. I will be completely aligned.

Sit with your hands in the Root Position for 5 to 10 minutes.

Section: 4 - Root – Element: Protect and Strengthen with Earth – Step: Visual Day 14

Now you have Opened, Cleansed, and Energized the Root Chakra. It is now strong and healthy. It is time to seal and protect the Root Chakra and make it strong.

Keep the Root Stone in your right hand and the Earth Stone in the left.

Lie on the earth outdoors on your stomach. Place a rock or a bit of soil on the base of your spine. Place your hands with palms facing upward. It's okay to let your hands rest on the ground.

Visualize that the energy from the earth on your spine is connecting with the ground beneath you. Straight through your body in a beam of red energy. It is securing you to the ground. With every in- and out-breath the earth's energy connects you to the ground and then moves back up again.. As the earth's energy moves through the Root Chakra, the chakra is growing into a white Heritage Rose. It's slowly growing with each breath one petal at a time. Four of the petals are Red. Once the Rose if fully bloomed it SLOWLY starts to spin in a circle. With each circle, it spins faster and faster. It is now glowing shiny-red and spinning energetically. The beam of light radiates as brightly as possible – almost blindingly bright for just a moment, then the beam sinks down through your body and into the ground SLOWLY, while your chakra still glows and spins. Now the energy from your own glowing spinning chakra gets brighter, and the red light slowly starts to fill your whole body. Remain like this for at least 10 minutes, longer you need to.

Section: 4 - Root

Element: Protect and Strengthen with

Earth Step: Prayer - Day 15

I pray for the Protection of God's earth. Let it strengthen my Root Chakra so that the feelings of fear and insecurity can never return. I want to stand on the earth's solid ground. I give thanks for the security it brings into my Root Chakra. I pray that the earth's security will always be deeply rooted in me. I am at home with the earth, and the earth is at home with me. I pray for the earth's grounding energy so that I can have the strength I need to move forward on the path that God has laid out for me. AMEN.

Section: 4 - Root– Element: Protect and Strengthen with Earth
Step: Crystal Healing, - Day 16

In a bowl, mix one cup of soil and one cup of rock salt with a half-cup of water (enough to make it muddy). Lie on your stomach and place the Root Stone on your spine. Put both hands on the floor facing palm up. Keep the Earth Stone in the opposite hand to your writing

hand. Remain like this for 5 minutes while the crystals open this chakra.

Now use your writing hand to dip the Root Stone in the soil mix. Make a large rectangle across your whole back, spreading the muddy soil from top to bottom of your back (as big as you can without straining, making sure to cross your tailbone at the bottom of the rectangle). Do this 50 times in a clockwise direction.

Now, leave the crystal near the base of your spine or in the small of your back, and rest your hand back down on the floor, palm up, for a few minutes.

When you are ready, take the crystal and move it in a small rectangle just around your tailbone. Do this 50 times.

Now sit up and take the Root Stone in your writing hand.

Put both hands in the Root Mudra Position. Both hands should now be in the Root Mudra Position, with the Root Stone in your writing hand and the Earth Stone in the other hand. Remain like this for at least 10 minutes, longer if necessary.

Section: 4 - Root

Element: Protect and Strengthen with Earth – Step: Ritual - Day - Day 17

Make a mixture of soil and rock salt. Surround yourself with it in a circle. Place the Earth Stone on the circle, directly in front of you, while holding the Root Stone in your hand. (Keep the Root Stone in the right hand while you wait for the chakra to open, then you can keep it in the hand that's most comfortable.) You'll need four pieces of paper. You are going to write one line on each paper.

1. May the earth be strong

2. and protect my Root Chakra.

3. By using the four elements

4. I will be completely aligned.

Now sit with your hands in the Root Chakra position for 5 to 10 minutes. Then bury the four pieces of paper in the ground outdoors.

Closing Day of the Root Chakra - Day 18

1. As you inhale, speak the first part of each phrase. 2. As you exhale, speak the second part of the phrase. 3. Repeat each of the twelve incantations 10 times.

(Inhale) My energy" – (Exhale) is free of blockages.

(Inhale) My root chakra" – (Exhale) is centered.

(Inhale) My Navel Chakra juices" – (Exhale) are passionate.

(Inhale) My solar plexus" – (Exhale) feels

confident.

(Inhale) My heart" – (Exhale) Gives and receives love.

(Inhale) My throat" – (Exhale) speaks the truth.

(Inhale) My third eye" – (Exhale) Sees past the physical world.

(Inhale) My Crown Chakra" – (Exhale) is full of wisdom.

(Inhale) My chakras" – (Exhale) are spinning in alignment.

(Inhale) I am" – (Exhale) centered and balanced.

Chapter two: Navel

Sanskrit Name: Swadhisthana

Chant: Vam

Location: Navel

Stones: Red Jasper, Garnet, Moonstone, Orange Tourmaline

Scent: Gardenia, Indian Paintbrush, Lady's Slipper, Hibiscus,

Color: Orange

Properties When Healed: Procreation, Polarity, Sensuality, Confidence, Sociability, Freedom, Movement

Properties When Over-Active: over-emotional, extremely attached to people

Properties When Under-Active: stiff, unemotional

Associated Body Parts: Ovaries, Testes, Womb, Kidneys, Urinary Tract, Skin, Spleen, Gallbladder, Recharges Etheric Body/Aura

Information Stored Inside Navel Chakra: duality, magnetism, controlling patterns, emotional feelings (joy, anger, fear)

Opening Day of the Navel - Day 19

1. As you inhale, speak the first part of the phrase. 2. As you exhale, speak the second part of the phrase. 3. Repeat each of the twelve incantations ten times.

(Inhale) My energy – (Exhale) is free of blockages.

(Inhale) My root chakra – (Exhale) is Centered.

(Inhale) My Navel Chakra juices – (Exhale) are Passionate.

(Inhale) My solar plexus – (Exhale) feels Confident.

(Inhale) My heart – (Exhale) Gives and receives love

(Inhale) My throat – (Exhale) speaks the truth.

(Inhale) My third eye – (Exhale) Sees past the physical world.

(Inhale) My Crown Chakra – (Exhale) is full of wisdom.

(Inhale) My chakras – (Exhale) are spinning in alignment.

(Inhale) I am – (Exhale) centered and balanced.

Section: 1 - Navel– Element: Opening with Air – Step: Visual - Day 20

We are going to do a Visual. To bring in the air element, you will do the visual next to a window, or outside in the fresh air. Put both hands in Navel Mudra Position. This will allow you to send energy into the Navel Chakra. Keep the Navel Stone in your right hand, and the Air Stone in the left.

Lay on your back on the floor or ground. Visualize a Orange Ball of Light hovering over you. Visualize a Orange Ball of Light hovering over your head. There is a tube that connects to the ball of light down to your belly button. As you breathe in you are taking in the energy from the ball of light above you, into the tube and straight into your chakra. Breathe in and hold it for 5 seconds. As your holding the light in your stomach your navel chakra BRUSTS with passionate energy spraying everywhere.. Breath in again and hold for 5 seconds. Again the navel bursts open with orange passionate energy. Keep doing this until you have inhaled a total of 10 times – or longer if you feel the need.

Section: 1 - Navel – Element: Opening with Air – Step: Prayer - Day 21

Today we will do a prayer to open the Navel Chakra.

You do not need any stones or tools.

I pray for the air to blow open the door to my Navel Chakra.

Blow away any obstacles that keep me from feeling passionate and lively.

Once this door is open I will do everything in my power to cleanse, energize, and protect it!

I pray for a burst of wind to shoot straight up through barriers that have been built up around my Navel Chakra.
No more will I feel unable to open up to people.
I will never feel stiff or unemotional like this again.
I will feel free and vibrant!
I pray to God to feel and hear the rush of the wind blowing through my open Navel Chakra! So that I can be open to those who love and care for me, and have the strength to keep moving forward on the path that God has laid out for me. Amen

Section: 1 - Navel – Element: Opening with Air – Step: Crystal healing - Day 22

Lie on your back in a place where you can feel a breeze. Place the Navel Stone on your stomach. Put both hands on the floor, palms upward. Hold the Air Stone in the opposite hand of your writing hand. Stay like this for 5 minutes while the crystals open the Navel Chakra

Then use your writing hand to move the Navel Stone in a line from your navel all the way up the center of your body to your breastbone. Do this 50 times.

Now leave the crystal on your navel, and rest your hand back down on the floor, palm up, for a few minutes. When you are ready, take the crystal and rub it in a circle around your navel. Make 50 circles.

Now sit up and hold the Navel Stone in your writing hand. Put both hands in the Navel Mudra Position. Both hands should now be in the Navel Mudra Position, with the Navel Stone in your writing hand, and the Air Stone in the other. Remain like this for at least 10 minutes, longer if needed.

Section: 1 - Navel – Element: Opening with Air – Step: Ritual - Day 23

Sit somewhere outside away from your home. A park or beach would do well. Bring seven bits of paper (or a large piece of paper that you can cut into seven pieces), a pen, a Navel Stone, an Air Stone, and some rock salt.

Place a ring of rock salt around you. Place the Air Stone on the ring of rock salt, directly in front of you, and keep the Navel Stone in your right hand.

Sit with your hands in the Navel Mudra Position while your Navel Chakra opens up.

Now write out the following seven lines, one line on each piece of paper. (You may keep the Navel Stone in the opposite of your writing hand while you copy the lines.) Place the first written line underneath the Air Crystal on the salt ring, and place the other lines following in a clockwise direction around the ring.

(It's okay for the paper to blow away after you place it around the circle.)

1. "May the Air burst through" – This line will go under the Air Stone in front of you.

2. "And open my Navel Chakra," – Place this line next in a clockwise direction.

3. "So I can Cleanse it with the water element," – Keep going around...

4. "Energize it with the fire element,"

5. "And Protect it with the earth element."

6. "By using the four elements"

7. "I will be completely aligned."

You may sit with your hands in the Navel Mudra Position again for 5 to 10 minutes. Then leave everything but the stones where they are – leave and do not look back.

Section: 2 - Navel– Element: Cleansing with Water – Step: Visual. - Day 24

To bring in the water element, you will perform the visual in a tub, the ocean, or a pool, lake, or anywhere that allows you to be at least half-submerged in water. Put both hands in Navel Mudra Position. This will allow you to send energy into the Navel Chakra. Keep the Navel Stone in your right hand, and the Water Stone in the left.

Sit down in the water and close your eyes. Visualize that the water you are submerged in is an Orange Sparkling Liquid for your spirit. When you are able to fully see the sparkling liquid in your mind's eye, take a breath in and out. Every time you breathe in, you are soaking up the liquid into your Navel Chakra. Hold it in for 5 seconds and let the navel chakra soak in the liquid. As you exhale, repeat "VAM" And let the liquid drain and rinse out completely. Keep repeating the steps until you have rinsed the chakra at least 10 times. Then allow the liquid to completely fill your body from head to toe. Now leave the water when you feel ready. Dry off completely and sit or stand with your hands in the Navel Mudra Position. Take your time to visualize the orange, creamy liquid you absorbed inside of your body as it is draining out.

After it has drained, you see that it has created a ball of light in your stomach. The orange liquid energy turns on the ball of light, and the light is spinning.

Every breath makes the light spin faster. Keep doing this for 10 minutes – or longer if you feel the need.

Section: 2 - Navel– Element: Cleansing with Water – Step: prayer - Day 25

I Pray to God for His cleansing holy water to pour though my Navel Chakra. Let it cleanse away all feelings of un-attachment to others. I want to bathe in that cleansing water and see all of the blackness that has been obstructing my Navel Chakra for so long clear out once and for all. I pray to feel clean and ready to fill the chakra with passion. I pray to feel the holy water filling me up inside and washing me inside and out.

I want it to wash away negative energy from my past and leave me feeling STRONGER! So that I can be Open and Vibrant and have the strength to keep moving forward on the path that God has laid out for me. Amen!

Section: 2 - Navel– Element: Cleansing with Water – Step: Crystal Healing - Day 26

Lie on your back with a bowl of rock-salt water close to you. Place the Navel Stone on your stomach. Put both hands faced

upward on the ground. Hold the Water Stone in the opposite hand to your writing hand.

Remain like this for 5 minutes while the crystals open this chakra.

Now use your writing hand to dip the Navel Stone in the water and move it from your Navel to your breastbone, in a wavy line. Allow yourself to feel the drip and wetness of the water on your skin. Do this 50 times. Now leave the crystal on your navel, and rest your hand back on the floor, palm up, for a few minutes.

When you are ready, take the crystal, dip it in the water, and move it in a wavy line across your body from one hip to the other and back again, crossing your navel in the middle. Do this 50 times. Sit up and hold the

Navel Stone in your writing hand. Put both hands in the Navel Mudra Position. Both hands should now be in the Navel Mudra Position, with the Navel Stone in your writing hand and the Water Stone in the other hand. Remain like this for at least 10 minutes – longer if needed.

Section: 2 - Navel– Element: Cleansing with Water – Step: Ritual - Day 27

Choose a place that has a lot of room, where you would not mind spilling lots of water – your backyard, a big round tub, or a hot tub would work well.

Mix one cup of rock salt with a gallon of water. Put the Water Stone and the Navel Stone in the gallon of salt water and let them soak for three hours.

Pour salt water into six cups or bowls.

(Dispose of any water remaining.)

Place the six cups around you in a circle. Place the Water Stone next to the cup front of you. Put your hands in the Navel Mudra Position, with the Navel Stone lying in your right hand for 5 minutes while the Navel Chakra opens.
Keep the Navel Stone in your right hand while you perform the following steps.

Repeat the next lines below, one by one. While you repeat the lines, you will pour one cup of water over your head for each line you repeat, starting with the cup in front of you and working clockwise. Repeat:

1. "May the Water Element rush through" – Pour the first cup in front of you over your head as you say this line. Pick up the next cup and repeat:

2. "And cleanse my Navel Chakra." Keep going around the circle of cups as you say each line. *3. "So I can Energize with the fire Element" 4. And Protect with the Earth element."*

5. "By using the four elements" 6. "I will be completely aligned." Stay in the circle for 5 to 10 minutes with your hands in the Navel Mudra Position and the Navel Stone in your right hand. Remain longer if needed.

Section: 3 - Navel– Element: Energizing with Fire – Step: Visual - Day 28

You may do this Visual with your hands in the Navel Mudra Position.

Hold the Fire Stone in your left hand and the Navel Stone in the right.

Visualize that every breath is igniting a little orange flame in your navel area.

With each breath, the orange flame grows bigger until it is a ball of orange fire in your stomach.

The orange fire is playful, vibrant, and passionate.

The fire ball starts to spin, and the energizing feeling increases.

I want you to fill in the blanks below with something in your life that you want to rid yourself of – whether it is a person, a habit, a house, a feeling inside of you – it can be ANYTHING! Inhale, hold in for 5 seconds. Let the fire increase in power. Once you feel like the pressure has built up enough, exhale.

Each time you exhale, visualize the fire striking out a flame in front of you to burn the negative word right up into ashes. Every time you EXHALE, the flame goes through your belly button and upward toward the spoken words.

(Inhale) "I am Open." – (Exhale) "I do not want_____."

(Inhale) "I am Passionate." – (Exhale) "I do not want_____."

(Inhale) "I am Expressive ." – (Exhale) "I do not want____."

(Inhale) "I am Lively." – (Exhale) "I do not want____."

Now you feel the fire slowing down until the Navel Chakra is glowing with a beautiful orange light. Repeat the final line:

(Inhale) "My Navel Chakra is energized ." (Exhale) "And it always will be."

Section: 3 - Navel– Element: Energizing with Fire – Step: Prayer - Day 29

I pray to God to feel the fire from the universe fiercely rushing through my Navel Chakra and energizing me.

I pray to feel the heat of the flame raise my vibration to a higher level.

I pray for the fire to energize my feeling of passion.

I pray for the fire to burn away anything that is keeping me from feeling open.

I pray for the fire to give me the ability to connect on a deeper level.

I pray for fire so I can see which way I am going and feel safe.

I have nothing to fear, because God has given me the Flame of Light.

I see who I am because of this light, and I love the person I see.

I allow the heat into my body completely. I openly allow it to burn away feelings of fear or insecurities. I am open with the Flame of Light, and it will energize my mind, body and soul. I pray for this flame so I can be Open and Passionate, and have the strength to keep moving forward on the path God that has laid out for me. Amen

Section: 3 - Navel – Element: Energizing with Fire – Step: Crystal Healing - Day 30

Leave the Fire Stone next to a lit orange or white candle for 3 hours.

Keep the lit candle next to you while you do this Crystal Healing.

Lie on your back, and place the Navel Stone on your stomach. Put both hands on the floor, palms upward. Hold the Fire Stone in the opposite hand to your writing hand.

Remain like this for 5 minutes while the crystals open the Navel Chakra

Now use your writing hand to move the Navel Stone in a big triangle on your stomach. The highest point of the triangle should be at the breastbone, and the two bottom corners should be at your hips at the level of the navel.

Do this 50 times in a clockwise direction.

Now leave the crystal on your navel and let your hands rest back on the floor, palms up for a few minutes.

When you are ready, hold the crystal and move it in a small triangle just around your navel. Do this 50 times.

Sit up and take the Navel Stone in your writing hand.

Put both hands in the Navel Mudra Position.

Both hands should now be in the Navel Mudra Position, with the Navel Stone in your writing hand and the Fire Stone in the other hand.

Remain like this for at least 10 minutes, or longer if needed.

Section: 3 - Navel – Element: Energizing with Fire – Step: Ritual - Day 31

Place five orange or white candles around you in a circle.

Place the Fire Stone next to the candle in front of you, and hold the Navel Stone in your right hand.

Sit with your hands in the Navel Mudra Position while your Navel Chakra opens up.

Now write out the following five lines, one line each on five pieces of paper. (You may

keep the Navel Stone in the opposite of your writing hand while you copy the lines.)
After you write the first line, burn it in the candle directly in front of you. Then write the next line and burn it in the candle next to it in a clockwise direction.
(You can keep a bowl or cup of water with you to put the bits of flaming paper for safety after the words have burned.)

1. "May the Fire element roar with heat and flame" – Burn the line in the candle flame in front of you.

2. "And energize my Navel Chakra" – Burn the line in the next candle.

3. "So I can protect it with the Earth Element" – And so on...

4. "By using the four elements"

5. "I will be completely aligned."

Sit with your hands in the Navel Mudra Position for 5 to 10 minutes, longer if you feel it's needed.

Section: 4 - Navel– Element: Protect and Strengthen with Earth – Step: Visual Day 32

Now you have opened, cleansed, and energized the Navel Chakra. It is now strong and healthy. It is time to seal and protect it, and make it strong.

Put both hands in Navel Mudra Position. This will allow you to send energy into the Navel Chakra. Keep the Navel Stone in your right hand and the Earth Stone in the Left.

Lie on the earth outdoors on your back. Place a rock or a bit of soil on your navel. Visualize that the energy from the earth on your stomach is connecting with the ground beneath you. Straight through your body in a beam of orange energy. It is securing you to the ground.

With every in- and out-breath the earth's energy connects you to the ground and then moves back up again.. As the earth's energy moves through the Navel Chakra, the chakra is growing into a White Hibiscus. The Flower is slowly blooming with each breath one petal at a time.

6 of the petals are Orange, Once the Flower is fully bloomed it starts to spin

The light from the earth on your stomach radiates as brightly as possible. It is almost blindingly bright for just a moment. Then its sinks down SLOWLY through your body and into the ground, while your Navel Chakra is still glowing and spinning.

Now the energy from your own glowing, spinning chakra gets brighter, and the orange light slowly begins to fill your entire body. Remain like this for at least 10 minutes – longer if needed.

Section: 4 - Navel

Element: Protect and Strengthen with

Earth Step: Prayer - Day 33

I pray for the Protection of 'God's earth. Let it strengthen my Navel Chakra so that the ridged and stiff feelings I had can never return. I want to stand on the earth's ground, and I can feel the life within it. I give thanks for the passion it brings into my Navel Chakra. I pray that the earth's lively energy will always be within me. The earth gives me unlimited physical energy, and I pray that it always will. I pray for the earth's passionate energy so that I can have the strength I need to move forward on the path that God has laid out for me.

Amen.

<u>Section: 4 - Navel – Element: Protect and Strengthen with Earth</u>

<u>Step: Crystal Healing - Day 34</u>

In a bowl, mix one cup of soil, one cup of rock salt, and half a cup of water (or just enough to make it muddy). Lie on your back and place the Navel Stone on your stomach. Put both hands faced upward on

the floor. Hold the Earth Stone in the opposite hand to your writing hand. Remain like this for 5 minutes while the crystals open this chakra.

Now use your writing hand to dip the Navel Stone in the soil mix. Make a large rectangle across your whole stomach, spreading the muddy soil downward across the breastbone along the center line of your stomach and then from hip to hip, crossing your navel. Do this 50 times in a clockwise direction.

Then leave the crystal on your navel and rest your hand back down on the floor, palm up for a few minutes.

When you are ready, hold the crystal, dip it in soil again, and move it in a small rectangle just around your navel. Do this 50 times.

Sit up and take the Navel Stone in your writing hand. Put both hands in the Navel Mudra Position. Both hands should now be in the Navel Mudra Position, with Navel Stone in your writing hand and Earth Stone in the other hand. Remain like this for at least 10 minutes, longer if needed.

Section: 4 - Navel– Element: Protect and Strengthen with Earth – Step: Ritual Day 35

Make a mixture of soil and rock salt. Surround yourself with it in a circle. Place the Earth Stone on the circle directly in front of you, and hold the Navel Stone in your right hand. Sit with your hands in the Navel Mudra Position while your Navel Chakra opens up.

Now write the following four lines, one line on each of four pieces of paper. (You may keep the Navel Stone in the opposite hand to your writing hand while you copy the lines.)

1. "May the earth be strong"

2. "And protect my Navel Chakra."

3. "By using the four elements"

4. "I will be completely aligned."

Now sit with your hands in the Navel Mudra Position for 5 to 10 minutes, longer if needed.

Then bury the four pieces of paper in the ground outside.

Closing Day of the Navel - Day 36

1. As you inhale, speak the first part of each phrase below. 2. As you exhale, speak the second part of the phrase. 3. Repeat each of the twelve incantations ten times.

(Inhale) "My energy" - (Exhale) "is free of blockages."

(Inhale) "My root chakra" - (Exhale) "is Centered."

(Inhale) "My Navel Chakra juices" - (Exhale) "are Passionate."

(Inhale) "My solar plexus" - (Exhale) "feels Confident."

(Inhale) "My heart" – (Exhale) "gives and receives love."

(Inhale) "My throat " – (Exhale) "speaks the truth."

(Inhale) "My third eye" – (Exhale) "sees past the physical world."

(Inhale) "My Crown Chakra" – (Exhale) "is full of wisdom."

(Inhale) "My chakras" – (Exhale) "are spinning in alignment."

(Inhale) "I am" – (Exhale) "centered and balanced."

Chapter three: Solar Plexus

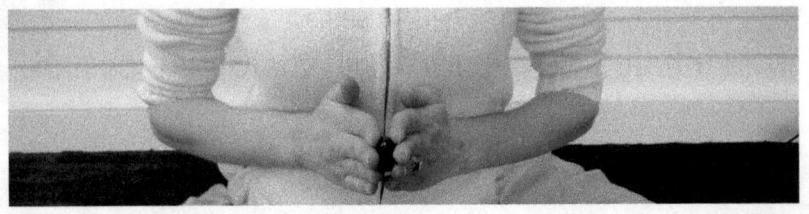

Sanskrit Name: Manipura

Chant: Ram

Location: Breastbone

Stones: Citrine, Jasper, Golden Topaz, Yellow Tourmaline

Scent: Cinnamon, Chamomile, Golden Yarrow, Peppermint

Color: Yellow

Properties when Healed: Personal Power, Will, Knowledge, Wit, Laughter, Mental Clarity, Humor, Optimism, Self-Control, Curiosity, Awareness

Properties when over-active: Domineering, Aggressive

Properties when under-active: Passive, Indecisive, Timid

Associated Body Parts: Digestion, Liver, Stomach, Diaphragm, Nervous System, Pancreas, Metabolism, Small Intestines

Information Stored Inside Solar Plexus Chakra: Personal power, Personality, Consciousness of Self Within the Universe (sense of belonging), Knowing

Opening Day of the Solar Plexus - Day 37

1. As you inhale, speak the first part of each phrase below. 2. As you exhale, speak the second part of the phrase. 3. Repeat each of the twelve incantations ten times.

(Inhale) "My energy" – (Exhale) "is free of blockages."

(Inhale) "My root chakra" – (Exhale) "is centered."

(Inhale) "My Navel Chakra juices" – (Exhale) "are Passionate."

(Inhale) "My solar plexus" – (Exhale) "feels confident."

(Inhale) "My heart" – (Exhale) "Gives and receives love."

(Inhale) "My throat" – (Exhale) "speaks the truth."

(Inhale) "My third eye" – (Exhale) "Sees past the physical world."

(Inhale) "My Crown Chakra" – "Exhale is full of wisdom."

(Inhale) "My chakras" – (Exhale) "are spinning in alignment."

(Inhale) "I am" – (Exhale) "centered and balanced."

Section: 1 - Solar Plexus – Element: Opening with Air – Step: Visual - Day 38

We are going to do a visual. To bring in the air element, you will do the visual next to a window or outside in the fresh air. Put both hands in Solar Plexus Mudra Position. This will allow you to send energy into the Solar Plexus Chakra. Keep the Solar Plexus and Air Stones between your hands.

Lay on your back on the floor or ground. Visualize a Yellow Ball of Light hovering over you. There is a tube that connects to the ball of light down to your Solar Plexus. As you breathe in you are taking in the energy from the ball of light above you, into the tube and straight into your chakra. Breathe in and hold it for 5 seconds. As your holding the light in your chest your solar plexus spins energetically fast and faster. Your chest fills with power and confidence. As you breathe out, the yellow energy is release in a beam of light shooting straight out of the top of your head. Breath in again and hold for 5 seconds. Again the Solar Plexus spins with powerful energy. Keep doing this until you have inhaled a total of 10 times – or longer if you feel the need.

Section: 1 - Solar Plexus – Element: Opening with Air – Step: Prayer - Day 39

I pray for the air to blow open the door to my Solar Plexus Chakra.

Blow away any obstacles that keep me from feeling confident and secure about myself.

Once this door is open, I will do everything in my power to cleanse, energize, and protect it!

I pray for a burst of wind to shoot straight up through barriers that have been raised around my Solar Plexus Chakra.
No more will I feel unsure about myself.
I will never feel unimportant or belittled again.
I will feel beautiful and powerful!

I pray to God to feel and hear the rush of the wind blowing through my open Solar Plexus Chakra! – so that I will have the inner power I need to accomplish my goals, and the strength to keep moving forward on the path that God has laid out for me. Amen

Section: 1 - Solar Plexus – Element: Opening with Air – Step: Crystal Healing

Day 40

Lie on your back in a place where you can feel a breeze. Place the Solar Plexus Stone on your breastbone. Put both hands on the floor, palms turned upward. Keep the Air Stone in the opposite hand to your writing hand. Remain like this for 5 minute while the crystals open this chakra.

Now use your writing hand to move the Solar Plexus Stone in a line downward from your breastbone all the way to your navel. Do this 50 times.

Leave the crystal on your Solar Plexus, and rest your hand back on the floor, palm up, for a few minutes.

When you are ready, hold the crystal and rub it in a circle around your Solar Plexus. Make 50 circles.

Then sit up and take the Solar Plexus Stone in your writing hand. Put both hands in the Solar Plexus Mudra Position.

Both hands should now be in the Solar Plexus Mudra Position, with the Solar Plexus and Air Stones held between your hands. Remain like this for at least 10 minutes, longer if needed.

<u>Section: 1 - Solar Plexus – Element: Opening with Air – Step: Ritual - Day 41</u>

Sit somewhere outdoors, away from your home. A park or beach will do well. Bring seven bits of paper (or a large piece of paper that you can cut into seven pieces) a pen, a Solar Plexus Stone, and an Air Stone.

Place a ring of rock salt around you. Place the Air Stone on the ring of salt, directly in front of you. Sit with your hands in the Solar Plexus Mudra Position, and hold the Solar Plexus Stone between your hands. Let the chakra open for 5 minutes.

Now, write out the following seven lines, one line on each of the seven pieces of paper. While you write, you can hold the stone in the opposite to your writing hand.

Place the first written line underneath the Air Crystal on the salt ring. Then place the other lines on the salt ring in a clockwise direction around the ring. It's okay if the air blows the paper away after you place it on the circle.

1. *"May the Air burst through"*

Place this line under the Air Stone in front of you.

2. *"and open my Solar Plexus Chakra."*

Place this line on the ring of rock salt in the next position clockwise.

*3. "So I can Cleanse with the water element," *– Keep going around...

4 "Energize with the fire element,"

5. "And Protect it with the earth element."

6 "By using the four elements"

7. "I will be completely aligned."

You may sit with you hands in the Solar Plexus Mudra Position again for 5 to 10 minutes. Then leave everything but the stones where they are – and leave and do not look back.

Section: 2 - Solar Plexus – Element: Cleansing with Water

Step: Visual - Day 42

To bring in the water element, you will perform the visual in a tub, the ocean, or a pool, lake, or any place that will allow you to be at least half submerged in water. Put both hands in the Solar Plexus Mudra Position. This will allow you to send energy into the Solar Plexus Chakra. Hold the Solar Plexus and Water Stones between your hands.

Sit down in the water and close your eyes. Visualize the water you are submerged as a Yellow Empowering Liquid for your spirit. When you are able to fully see the Empowering Liquid in your mind's eye, breathe in and out. Every time you breathe in, you are soaking up the liquid into your Solar Plexus Chakra.

Hold it in for 5 seconds and let the solar plexus chakra soak in the liquid. As you exhale, repeat "RAM"

And let the liquid drain and rinse out completely. Keep repeating the steps until you have rinsed the chakra at least 10 times.

Then allow the liquid to completely fill your body from head to toe.

When you feel ready, leave the water, dry off completely, and sit or stand with your hands in the Solar Plexus Mudra Position. Take time to visualize the yellow liquid that you absorbed inside your body, as it drains out of your open chakra.

After it has drained out, you see that it has created a ball of light in your breastbone area, and that the light is spinning around the ball. Every breath makes the light spin faster. Keep doing this for 10 minutes – or longer if you feel the need.

Section: 2 - Solar Plexus

Element: Cleansing with Water

Step: Prayer - Day 43

I pray to God for His cleansing holy water to pour though my Solar Plexus Chakra.

Let it cleanse away all feelings of unworthiness.

I want to bathe in the cleansing water and see all the blackness that has obstructed my Solar Plexus Chakra for so long clear out once and for all.

I pray to feel clean and ready to fill the chakra with unlimited energizing power.

I pray to feel the holy water filling me inside, and washing me inside and out. I want it to wash away negative energy from my past. I want the holy water to leave me feeling STRONGER! So that I can be Confident and Powerful and have the strength to keep moving forward on the path that God has laid out for me.

Amen!

Section: 2 - Solar Plexus – Element: Cleansing with Water

Step: Crystal Healing - Day 44

Lie on your back with a bowl of rock salt water close to you. Place the Solar Plexus Stone on your breastbone. Place both hands palms upward on the ground. Keep the Water Stone in the opposite hand to your writing hand.

Remain like this for 5 minutes while the stones open this chakra.

Now use your writing hand to dip the Solar Plexus Stone in the holy water and move it in a wavy line from your solar plexus to your navel. Allow yourself to feel the drip and wetness of the water on your skin. Do this 50 times.

Leave the crystal on your solar plexus. Rest your hand back on the floor for a few minutes, palm up.

When you are ready, take the crystal, dip it in the water, and move it in a wavy line across your body from one rib to the other and back again, crossing your solar plexus in the middle.

Do this 50 times.

Sit up and take the Solar Plexus Stone in your writing hand.

Put both hands in the Solar Plexus Mudra Position.

Both hands should now be in the Solar Plexus Mudra Position, with the Solar Plexus and Water Stones held between your hands. Remain like this for at least 10 minutes, longer if you feel the need.

Section: 2 - Solar Plexus– Element: Cleansing with Water – Step: Ritual

Day 45

Choose a place that has lots of room, where you will not mind spilling a lot of water – a backyard, a big round tub, or a hot tub will work well. Mix one cup of rock salt with a gallon of water. Put the Water Stone and the Solar Plexus Stone in the gallon of saltwater and let it soak for three hours. Pour the salt water into six cups or bowls. (Dispose of whatever water remains.)

Place the six cups around you in a circle. Place the Water Stone in front of you on the circle. Sit with your hands in the Solar Plexus Mudra Position, and hold the Solar Plexus Stone between your hands. Let the chakra open for 5 minutes. Keep the Navel Stone in your right hand while you follow the next steps.

Repeat the following six lines one by one. While you repeating each line, pour one cup of water over your head, starting with the cup in front of you and working clockwise.

Repeat: *1. "May the Water Element rush through"* – Pour the cup in front of you over your head as you say this line.

2. "And Cleanse my Solar Plexus Chakra." Keep going around the circle, pouring a cup as you say the next line.

3 "So I can Energize with the fire Element"

4 "And Protect with the Earth element."

5 "By using the four elements"

6. "I will be completely aligned." Remain in the circle for 5 to 10 minutes with your hands in the Solar Plexus Mudra Position and the Solar Plexus Stone held in your right hand. Remain longer if you feel the need to.

Section: 3 - Solar Plexus– Element: Energizing with Fire – Step: Visual
Day 46

Put both hands in Solar Plexus Mudra Position. This will allow you to send energy into the Solar Plexus Chakra. Hold the Solar Plexus and Fire Stones between your hands.

Visualize that every breath is igniting a small Yellow flame in the area of your breastbone.

With each breath, the Yellow flame grows larger, until it is a ball of Yellow fire in your solar plexus. The fire is powerful and strong. The ball of fire begins to spin, and the feeling of power increases.

Fill in the blanks below with something in your life that you want to rid yourself of, whether it is a person, a habit, a house, a feeling inside of you – ANYTHING! Inhale, hold in for 5 seconds. Let the fire increase in power. Once you feel like the pressure has built up enough, exhale.

Every time you exhale, visualize the fire striking a flame out in front of you to burn the negative word right up into ashes. The flame goes through your breastbone and upward toward the spoken words each time you EXHALE.

(Inhale) "I am Confident." (Exhale) "I do not want_____."

(Inhale) "I am a Leader." (Exhale) "I do not want_____."

(Inhale) "I am Powerful." – (Exhale) "I do not want____."

(Inhale) "I am Beautiful." – (Exhale) "I do not want____."

Now you feel the fire slow down until the Solar Plexus Chakra is glowing with a beautiful Yellow light. Repeat:

(Inhale) "My Solar Plexus Chakra is energized" EXHALE" – "and it always will be."

Section: 3 - Solar Plexus– Element: Energizing with Fire – Step: Prayer
Day 47

I pray to God to feel the fire from the universe fiercely rushing through my Solar Plexus Chakra and energizing me.

I pray to feel the heat of the flame raise my vibration to a higher level. I pray for the fire to energize my feeling of confidence. I pray for the fire to burn away anything that is keeping me from feeling beautiful. I pray for the fire to give me the ability to lead others forward. I pray for fire to help me see which way I am heading, and feel safe as I move onward. I have nothing to fear, because God has given me the flame of light. I see my inner power because of this light, and I know that it is inside of me now. I allow the heat to come into my body completely, and I confidently allow it to burn away feelings of unworthiness or insecurities. I am open with the flame of light, and it will energize my mind, body, and soul. I pray that flame enable me to be inspiring and powerful and have the strength to keep moving forward on the path that God has laid out for me. Amen

Section: 3 - Solar Plexus– Element: Energizing with Fire

Step: Crystal Healing - Day 48

Place the Fire Stone next to a lit yellow or white candle and leave it there for 3 hours.

Keep the lit candle next to you while you do this Crystal Healing.

Lie on your back and place the Solar Plexus Stone on your breastbone. Rest both hands on the floor, palms upward.

Keep the Fire Stone in the opposite hand to your writing hand. Remain like this for 5 minutes while the crystals open this chakra.

Now use your writing hand to move the Solar Plexus Stone in a large triangle on your stomach. The highest point of the triangle is your breastbone, and the two bottom corners are your hips. Do this 50 times in a clockwise direction.

Then leave the crystal on your Solar Plexus, and rest your hand palm-up on the floor for a few minutes.

When you are ready, take the crystal and move it in a small triangle just around your solar plexus. Do this 50 times.

Sit up and hold the Solar Plexus Stone in your writing hand.

Put both hands in the Solar Plexus Mudra Position.

Both hands should now be in the Solar Plexus Mudra Position, with the Solar

Plexus and Fire Stones held between your hands.

Remain like this for at least 10 minutes, longer if needed.

Section: 3 - Solar Plexus– Element: Energizing with Fire – Step: Ritual Day 49

Place five yellow or white candles around you in a circle.

Place the Fire Stone next to the candle in front of you.

Sit with your hands in the Solar Plexus Mudra Position, and hold the Solar

Plexus Stone in between your hands. Let the chakra open for 5 minutes. Keep the Navel Stone in either hand that is comfortable while you follow the next steps.

You will write out five lines, one line on each of five pieces of paper. After you write the first line, you will burn it in the candle directly in front of you. Then write the next line and burn it in the next candle in the clockwise direction.

(You can keep a bowl or cup of water nearby to put the flaming paper after the words have burned.)

1. *"May the Fire element roar with heat and flame"* – Burn in candle in front of you.
2. *"And energize my Solar Plexus Chakra."* – Burn in the next candle.
3. *"So I can protect it with the Earth Element."* – And so on...
4. *"By using the four elements"*
5. *"I will be completely aligned.*

Sit with your hands in the Solar Plexus Position for 5 to 10 minutes, longer if needed.

Section: 4 - Solar Plexus – Element: Protect and Strengthen with Earth Step: Visual - Day 50

You have now Opened, Cleansed, and Energized the Solar Plexus Chakra. It is now strong and healthy. It is time to seal and protect it and make it strong.

Put both hands in Solar Plexus Mudra Position. This will allow you to send energy into the Solar Plexus Chakra. Hold the Solar Plexus and Earth Stones between your hands.

Lie on the earth outdoors on your back. Place a rock or a bit of soil on your Solar Plexus. Visualize that the energy from the earth on your stomach is connecting with the ground beneath you. Straight through your body in a beam of Yellow energy. It is securing you to the ground.

With every in- and out-breath the earth's energy connects you to the ground and then moves back up again..

As the earth's energy moves through the Solar Plexus Chakra, the chakra is growing into a White Richelieu Rose. The Flower is slowly blooming with each breath one petal at a time. 10 of the petals are yellow, Once the Flower is fully bloomed it starts to spin The light from the earth on your solar plexus radiates as brightly as possible. It is almost blindingly bright for just a moment. Then its sinks down SLOWLY through your body and into the ground, while your solar plexus Chakra is still glowing and spinning. Now the energy from your own glowing, spinning chakra gets brighter, and the yellow light slowly begins to fill your entire body. Remain like this for at least 10 minutes, longer if needed.

Section: 4 - Solar Plexus – Element: Protect and Strengthen with Earth

Step: Prayer - Day 51

I pray for the protection of 'God's earth.

Let it strengthen my Solar Plexus Chakra so that the insecurity I once had can never return. I want to stand on the earth's powerful ground.

I give thanks for the encouragement that it brings into my Solar Plexus Chakra. I pray that the earth's strong energy will always be within me. The earth gives me unlimited confidence, and I pray that it always will. I pray for the earth's power, so that I can have the strength I need to move forward on the path that God has laid out for me.

Amen.

Section: 4 - Solar Plexus – Element: Protect and Strengthen with Earth
Step: Crystal Healing - Day 52

In a bowl, mix one cup of soil, one cup of rock salt, and half a cup of water (or enough to make it muddy). Lie on your back, and place the Solar Plexus Stone on your breastbone. Rest both hands on the ground, palms upward. Hold the Earth Stone in the opposite hand to your writing hand. Remain like this for 5 minutes while the crystals open this chakra.

Now use your writing hand to dip the Solar Plexus Stone in the soil mix. Make a large rectangle across your entire stomach, spreading the muddy soil from rib to rib, crossing the breastbone, then downward and from hip to hip. Do this 50 times in a clockwise direction.

Leave the crystal on your Solar Plexus and rest your hand on the floor, palm up, for a few minutes. When you are ready, take the crystal, dip it in the soil again, and move it in a small rectangle just around your Solar Plexus. Do this 50 times.

Sit up and hold the Solar Plexus Stone in your writing hand.

Put both hands in the Solar Plexus Mudra Position.

Both hands should now be in the Solar Plexus Mudra Position, with the Solar Plexus and Earth Stones held between your hands. Remain like this for at least 10 minutes, longer if needed.

Section: 4 - Solar Plexus – Element: Protect and Strengthen with Earth
Step: Ritual - Day 53

Make a mixture of soil and rock salt. Use the mixture to make a circle on the ground around you.

Place the Earth Stone on the circle directly in front of you. Sit with your hands in the Solar Plexus Mudra Position, and hold the Solar Plexus Stone between your hands. Let the chakra open for 5 minutes. Keep the Navel Stone in either hand while you follow the next steps.

You'll need four pieces of paper, and you will write one line on each piece of paper.

1. "May the earth be strong"

2. "and protect my Solar Plexus Chakra."

3. "By using the four elements"

4. "I will be completely aligned."

Now sit with your hands in the Solar Plexus Chakra position for 5 to 10 minutes – longer if Needed.

Then bury the four pieces of paper in the ground outside.

Closing Day of the Solar Plexus - Day 54

1. As you inhale, speak the first part of each phrase below. 2. As you exhale, speak the second part of the phrase. 3. Repeat each of the 12 incantations 10 times.

(Inhale) "My energy" – (Exhale) "is free of blockages."

(Inhale) "My root chakra" – (Exhale) "is Centered."

(Inhale) "My Navel Chakra juices" – (Exhale) "are Passionate."

(Inhale) "My solar plexus" – (Exhale) "feels Confident."

(Inhale) "My heart" – (Exhale) "Gives and receives love."

(Inhale) "My throat" – (Exhale) "speaks the truth."

(Inhale) "My third eye" – (Exhale) "Sees past the physical world."

(Inhale) "My Crown Chakra" – (Exhale) "is full of wisdom."

(Inhale) "My chakras" – (Exhale) "are spinning in alignment."

(Inhale) "I am" – (Exhale) "centered and balanced."

Chapter four: Heart

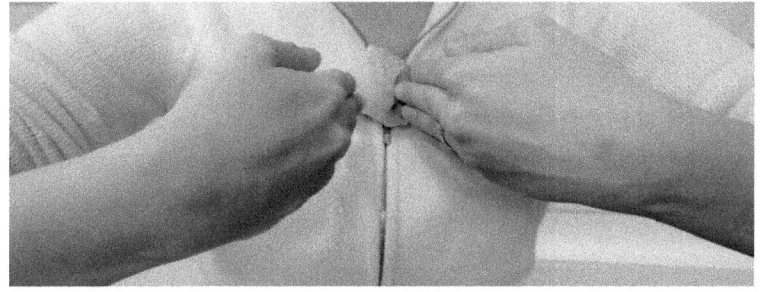

Sanskrit Name: Anahata

Chant: Yam

Location: Center of Chest

Stones: Aventurine, Malachite, Emerald, Rose Quartz

Scent: Jasmine, Holly, Poppy, California Wild Rose

Color: Green or Pink

Properties when Healed: Love, Acceptance, Self-Control, Compassion, Forgiveness, Harmony, Peace, Renewal, Growth

Properties when over-active: Suffocating Love, Selfishness

Properties when Under-active: Cold, Distant

Associated Body Parts: Lungs, Heart, Thymus Gland, Arms, Hands, Respiratory, Hypertension, Muscles

Information Stored Inside Heart Chakra: Connections or "heart strings" to those whom we love

Opening Day of the Heart - Day 55

1. As you inhale, speak the first part of the phrase. 2. As you exhale, speak the second part of the phrase. 3. Repeat each of the twelve incantations 10 times.

(Inhale) "My energy" – (Exhale) "is free of blockages."

(Inhale) "My root chakra" – (Exhale) "is Centered."

(Inhale) "My Navel Chakra juices" – (Exhale) "are Passionate."

(Inhale) "My solar plexus" – (Exhale) "feels Confident."

(Inhale) "My heart" – (Exhale) "Gives and receives love."

(Inhale) "My throat" – (Exhale) "speaks the truth."

(Inhale) "My third eye" – (Exhale) "Sees past the physical world."

(Inhale) "My Crown Chakra" – (Exhale) "is full of wisdom."

(Inhale) "My chakras" – (Exhale) "are spinning in alignment."

(Inhale) "I am" – (Exhale) "centered and balanced."

Section: 1 - Heart – Element: Opening with Air – Step: Visual - Day 56

We will do a visual. To bring in the air element, do the visual next to a window or outside in the fresh air. Put both hands in Heart Mudra Position. This will allow you to send energy into the Heart Chakra. Keep the Heart Stone and Air Stone held securely to your chest with your fingertips.

Lay on your back on the floor or ground. Visualize a Green Ball of Light hovering over you. There is a tube that connects to the ball of light down to your chest. As you breathe in you are taking in the energy from the ball of light above you, into the tube and straight into your chakra. Breathe in and hold it for 5 seconds. As your holding the light in your chest your heart chakra glows with a beautiful green energy that gets brighter and brighter. As you breathe out the green energy escapes out of your mouth and back into the ball of light above you Breath in again and hold for 5 seconds. Again the heart glows with green energy.Release it back out again. You are giving and receiving energy equally from and into your heart chakra. Keep doing this until you have inhaled a total of 10 times – or longer if you feel the need.

Section: 1 - Heart– Element: Opening with Air – Step: Prayer - Day 57

I pray for the air to blow open the door to my Heart Chakra.

Blow away any obstacles that keep me from giving and receiving love.

Once this door is open, I will do everything in my power to cleanse, energize, and protect it!
I pray for a burst of wind to shoot straight up through the barriers that have been put up around my Heart Chakra.
No more will I feel unable to love or be loved.
I will never feel this emptiness inside again.
I will laugh and feel joy!
I pray to God to feel and hear the rush of the wind blowing through my open Heart Chakra, so that I can love those who love and care for me.

I pray to have the strength to keep moving forward on the path that God has laid out for me. Amen

Section: 1 - Heart
Element: Opening with Air
Step: Crystal Healing - Day 58

Lie on your back where you can feel a breeze. Place the Heart Stone on your chest. Rest both hands on the ground, palms upward. Hold the Air Stone in the opposite hand to your writing hand.

Remain like this for 5 minute while the crystals open this chakra.

Now, use your writing hand to move the Heart Stone in a line from your Heart Chakra all the way down to your navel. Do this 50 times. Leave the crystal on your Heart, and rest your hand back on the floor, palm up, for a few minutes.

When you are ready, take the crystal and rub it in a circle around your Heart Chakra. Make 50 circles.

Sit up and take the Heart Stone in your writing hand. Put both hands in the Heart

Mudra Position. Both hands should now be in the Heart Mudra Position, with the Heart and Air Stones held securely to your chest with your fingertips. Remain like this for at least 10 minutes, longer if needed.

Section: 1 - Heart– Element: Opening with Air – Step: Ritual - Day 59

Sit somewhere outside away from your home. A park or a beach would do well. Bring a pen, a Heart Stone, an Air Stone, and seven bits of paper (or a large piece of paper that you can cut into seven pieces).

Place a ring of rock salt around you. Place the Air Stone on the ring of salt, directly in front of you. Sit with your hands in the Heart Mudra Position for about 5 minutes, letting your fingertips hold the Heart Stone to your chest while your Heart Chakra opens up.

Now, write the following seven lines, one on each piece of paper. (You may keep the Heart Stone in either hand that is comfortable while writing.) Place the first piece of paper with a written line under the Air Crystal on the salt ring, and place the others in a clockwise position around the ring. (It's okay if the air blows the paper away after you place it in the circle.)

1. *"May the Air burst through"* – This paper and written line will go under the Air Stone in front of you.

2. *"and open my Heart Chakra"* – Place this paper next in a clockwise direction.

3. *"So I can Cleanse with the water element"* – Keep going around…

4. *"Energize with the fire element,"*

5. *"And Protect it with the earth element."*

6. *"By using the four elements"*

7. *"I will be completely aligned."*

You may sit with your hands in the Heart Mudra Position again for 5 to 10 minutes. Finally, leave everything but the stones where they are – leave and do not look back.

Section: 2 - Heart - Element: Cleansing with Water – Step: Visual - Day 60

To bring in the water element, you will do this visual in a tub, the ocean, a pool, lake, or anywhere that will allow you to be at least half-submerged in water.

Put both hands in Heart Mudra Position. This will allow you to send energy into the Heart Chakra. Keep the Heart Stone and Water Stone held securely to your chest with your fingertips.

While sitting in the water, visualize the water you are submerged in as a green Healing Liquid for your spirit. It is Liquid Love. When you are able to fully see the Healing Liquid in your mind's eye, take a breath in and out. Every time you breathe in, you are soaking up the liquid into your Heart Chakra. Hold it in for 5 seconds and let the heart chakra soak in the liquid. As you exhale, repeat "YAM" And let the liquid drain and rinse out completely. Keep repeating the steps until you have rinsed the chakra at least 10 times. Then allow the liquid to completely fill your body from head to toe. Leave the water when you feel ready, dry off completely, and sit or stand with your hands in the Heart Mudra Position. Take time to visualize the Green creamy liquid that you absorbed inside of your body as it drains out. After it has drained out, you see that it has created a ball of light in your chest for the light to turn on, and the light is spinning. Every breath is making the light spin faster. Keep doing this for 10 minutes, or longer if needed.

Section: 2 - Heart– Element: Cleansing with Water – Step: Prayer - Day 61

I Pray to God for His cleansing holy water to pour though my Heart Chakra. Let it cleanse away all feelings of hate.

I want to bathe in the cleansing water and see all the blackness that has been obstructing my Heart Chakra for so long

clear out once and for all.

I pray to feel clean and ready to fill the

Heart Chakra with unlimited forgiving

energy.

I pray to feel the holy water filling me up

inside and washing me inside and out.

I want it to wash away negative energy from

my past and leave me feeling STRONGER!

So that I can be loving and nurturing, and

have the strength to keep moving forward on

the path that God has laid out for me.

Amen!

Section: 2 - Heart – Element: Cleansing with Water – Step: Crystal Healing
Day 62

Lie on your back with a bowl of rock salt water close to you. Place the Heart Stone on your Heart Chakra. Rest both hands palms upward on the ground. Hold the Water Stone in the opposite hand to your writing hand.

Remain like this for 5 minute while the crystals open this chakra.

Now use your writing hand to dip the Heart Stone in the water. Move it from your Heart Chakra to your navel in a wavy line. Allow yourself to feel the drip and wetness of the water on your skin.

Do this 50 times.

Then leave the crystal on your heart, and rest your hand back down on the floor, palm up, for a few minutes.

When you are ready, take the crystal, dip it in the water, and move it in a wavy line across your chest from one shoulder to the other and back again, crossing your heart in the middle.

Do this 50 times.

Sit up and hold the Heart Stone in your writing hand.

Put both hands in the Heart Mudra Position.

Both hands should now be in the Heart Mudra Position, with the Heart and Water Stones held securely to your chest with your fingertips.

Remain like this for at least 10 minutes, longer if needed.

Section: 2 - Heart – Element: Cleansing with Water – Step: Ritual - Day 3

You'll need to pick a place that has lots of room, where you won't mind spilling lots of water. Your backyard or a big round tub or hot tub would work nicely.

Mix one cup of rock salt with a gallon of water.

Put the Water Stone and the Heart Stone in the gallon of salt water and let it soak for three hours. Pour salt water into six cups or bowls.

(Dispose of any remaining water.)

Place the six cups around you in a circle. Place the Water Stone next to the cup in front of you. Sit with your hands in the Heart Mudra Position for about 5 minutes, letting your fingertips hold the Heart Stone to your chest while your Heart Chakra opens up.

Repeat the next six lines, one by one. As you repeat each line, you will pour one cup of water over your head, starting with the cup in front of you and working clockwise. (Hold the Heart Stone in your right hand.)

1. *"May the Water Element rush through"*

Pour the first cup in front of you over your head while you say this.

2. *"And Cleanse my Heart Chakra."*

Then keep going around the circle clockwise and pour a cup as you say the next line.

3. *"So I can Energize with the fire Element"*

4. *"And Protect with the Earth element."*

5. *"By using the four elements"*

6. *"I will be completely aligned."*

Remain in the circle for 5 to 10 minutes with your hands in the Heart Mudra Position and the Heart Stone held securely to your chest with your fingertips – stay longer if needed.

Section: 3 - Heart – Element: Energizing with Fire – Step: Visual - Day 64

Put both hands in Heart Mudra Position. This will allow you to send energy into the Heart Chakra. Hold the Heart Stone and Fire Stone securely to your chest with your fingertips.

Visualize that every breath is igniting a small Green flame in the area of the Heart Chakra.

With each breath, the Green flame becomes bigger until it is a ball of Green fire in your chest.

This fire is a Loving Friend.

The fire ball starts to spin, and the energizing feeling increases.

I want you to fill in each of the blanks below with something in your life that you want to rid yourself of, whether it is a person, a habit, a house, a feeling inside of you, ANYTHING! Inhale, hold in for 5 seconds. Let the fire increase in power. Once you feel like the pressure has built up enough, exhale.

Every time you exhale, visualize the fire striking out a flame in front of you to burn the negative word right up into ashes. The flame goes through your Heart Chakra and rises up toward the spoken words every time you exhale.

(Inhale) "I am loving" – (Exhale) "I do not want_____."

(Inhale) "I am forgiving" – (Exhale) "I do not want_____."

(Inhale) "I am open" – (Exhale) "I do not want ___."

(Inhale) "I am friendly" – (Exhale) "I do not want ___."

Now you feel the fire slowing down until the Heart Chakra is just glowing with a beautiful Green light.

Repeat:

(Inhale) "My Heart Chakra is energized" – (Exhale) "and it always will be."

Section: 3 - Heart – Element: Energizing with Fire – Step: Prayer - Day 65

I pray to God to feel the fire from the universe fiercely rushing through my Heart Chakra and energizing me.

I pray to feel the heat of the flame raise my vibration to a higher level.

I pray for the fire to energize my feelings of love for others.

I pray for the fire to burn away anything that is keeping me from feeling open.

I pray for the fire to give me the ability to connect on a deeper level.

I pray for fire to help me see the true intentions of others and feel safe.

I have nothing to fear, because God has given me the flame of light.

I am not afraid of opening my heart, because the flame allows me to see how loved I am.

I allow the heat into my body completely, and I openly allow it to burn away feelings of fear or hate. I am open with the Flame of Light, and it will energize my mind, body, and soul. I pray for this flame so that I can love, and laugh, and have the strength to keep moving forward on the path that God has laid out for me. Amen

Section: 3 - Heart– Element: Energizing with Fire – Step: Crystal Healing

Day 66

Leave the Fire Stone next to a lit green or white candle for three hours.

Keep the lit candle next to you while you do this Crystal Healing.

Lie on your back, and place the Heart Stone on your Heart Chakra. Rest both

**hands palms upward on the ground. Hold the Earth Stone in the opposite hand to your writing hand.
Remain like this for 5 minutes, while the crystals open this chakra.**

Now use your writing hand to move the Heart Stone in a big triangle on your chest. The highest point of the triangle is your Heart Chakra, and the two bottom corners are your hips.
Do this 50 times in a clockwise direction.

Leave the crystal on your heart, and rest your hand back on the floor, palm up, for a few minutes. When you are ready, take the crystal and move it in a small triangle just around your heart. Do this 50 times.

Sit up and take the Heart Stone in your writing hand. Put both hands in the Heart Mudra Position.

Both hands should now be in the Heart Mudra Position, with the Heart and Fire Stones held securely to your chest with your fingertips.

Remain like this for at least 10 minutes, longer if needed.

Section: 3 - Heart – Element: Energizing with Fire – Step: Ritual

Day 67

Place five green or white candles around you in a circle.

Place the Fire Stone next to the candle in front of you

Sit with your hands in the Heart Mudra Position for about 5 minutes, letting your

fingertips hold the Heart Stone to your chest while your Heart Chakra opens up.

Now, write out the following five lines, one on each of five pieces of paper. (You may hold the Heart Stone in either hand that is comfortable while you write.) After you write the first line, you will burn it in the candle directly in front of you. Then write the next line and burn it in the next candle next in a clockwise direction. (You can keep a bowl or cup of water with you to put the bit of flaming paper in for safety after the words have burned.)

1. *"May the Fire element roar with heat and flame"* Burn this line in the candle in front of you.

2. *"And Energize my Heart Chakra"* - Burn this line in the next candle…

3. *"So I can protect it with the Earth Element"* – And so on...

4. *"By using the four elements"*

5. *"I will be completely aligned."*

Sit with your hands in the Heart Position with the Heart Stone held securely to your chest with your fingertips for 5 to 10 minutes, longer if needed.

Section: 4 - Heart– Element: Protect and Strengthen with Earth – Step: Visual

Day 68

Now you have Opened, Cleansed, and Energized the Heart Chakra. It is now strong and healthy. It is time to seal and protect it, and make it strong.

Put both hands in the Heart Mudra Position. This will allow you to send energy into the Heart Chakra. Keep the Heart Stone and Air Stone held securely to your chest with your fingertips.

Lie on the earth outdoors on your back. Place a rock or a bit of soil on your Heart Chakra. Visualize that the energy from the earth on your chest is connecting with the ground beneath you. Straight through your body in a beam of Green energy. It is securing you to the ground.

With every in- and out-breath the earth's energy connects you to the ground and then moves back up again..

As the earth's energy moves through the Heart Chakra, the chakra is growing into a White Chamomile.

The Flower is slowly blooming with each breath one petal at a time. 12 of the petals are green, Once the Flower is fully bloomed it starts to spin The light from the earth on your stomach radiates as brightly as possible. It is almost blindingly bright for just a moment. Then its sinks down SLOWLY through your body and into the ground, while your Heart Chakra is still glowing and spinning. Now the energy from your own glowing, spinning chakra gets brighter, and the green light slowly begins to fill your entire body. Remain like this for at least 10 minutes, longer if needed.

Section: 4 - Heart– Element: Protect and Strengthen with Earth – Step: Prayer
Day 69

I pray for the Protection of 'God's earth.

Let it strengthen my Heart Chakra so that the hateful feelings I once had can never return.

I want to stand on the earth's loving ground.

I give thanks for the joy it brings into my Heart Chakra.

I pray that the earth's joyful energy will always be within me.

The earth gives me an unlimited amount of unconditional love, and I pray that it always will.

I pray for the earth's love so that I can have the strength I need to move forward on the path that God has laid out for me.

Amen.

Section: 4 - Heart– Element: Protect and Strengthen with Earth – Step: Crystal Healing - Day 70

Mix in a bowl one cup of soil, one cup of rock salt, and half a cup of water (or enough to make it muddy).

Lie on your back, and place the Heart Stone on your Heart Chakra. Rest both hands palms upward on the ground. Hold the Earth Stone in the opposite hand to your writing hand.

Remain like this for 5 minutes while the crystals open this chakra.

Now use your writing hand to dip the Heart Stone in the soil mix. Make a large rectangle across your entire chest, spreading the muddy soil from shoulder to shoulder, crossing your heart, then downward and from hip to hip. Do this 50 times in a clockwise direction.

Leave the crystal on your heart and rest your hand back down on the floor, palm up, for a few minutes.

When you are ready, take the crystal and move it in a small rectangle just around your heart. Do this 50 times.

Sit up and take the Heart Stone in your writing hand.

Put both hands in the Heart Mudra Position.

Both hands should now be in the Heart Mudra Position, with the Heart and Earth Stones held securely to your chest with your fingertips.

Remain like this for at least 10 minutes, longer if needed.

Section: 4 - Heart– Element: Protect and Strengthen with Earth – Step: Ritual Day 71

Make a mixture of soil and rock salt. Surround yourself with it in a circle. Place the Earth Stone on the circle, directly in front of you. Sit with your hands in the Heart Mudra Position for about five minutes, letting your fingertips hold the Heart Stone to your chest while your Heart Chakra opens up..

You'll need four pieces of paper. Write the following four lines, one on each the four pieces of paper. (You may hold the Heart Stone in either hand that is comfortable while you write.)

1. *"May the earth be strong"*
2. *"And protect my Heart Chakra."*
3. *"By using the four elements"*
4. *"I will be completely aligned."*

Now sit with your hands in the Heart Chakra position for 5 to 10 minutes, with the Heart Stone held securely to your chest – longer if needed. Bury the four pieces of paper in the ground outside.

Closing Day of the Heart - Day 72

1. As you inhale, speak the first part of the phrase. 2. As you exhale, speak the second part of the phrase. 3. Repeat each of the twelve incantations ten times.

(Inhale) "My energy" – (Exhale) "is free of blockages."

(Inhale) "My root chakra" – (Exhale) "is Centered."

(Inhale) "My Navel Chakra juices" – (Exhale) "are Passionate."

(Inhale) "My solar plexus" – (Exhale) "feels Confident."

(Inhale) "My heart" – (Exhale) "Gives and receives love."

(Inhale) "My throat" – (Exhale) "speaks the truth."

(Inhale) "My third eye" – (Exhale) "Sees past the physical world."

(Inhale) "My Crown Chakra" – (Exhale) "is full of wisdom."

(Inhale) "My chakras" – (Exhale) "are spinning in alignment."

Inhale I am" – (Exhale) "centered and balanced."

Chapter five: Throat

Sanskrit Name: Vishuddha

Chant: Ham

Location: Throat, Neck Region

Stones: Angelite, Chrysocolla, Blue Opal

Scent: Citrus, Cosmos, Trumpet Vine, Larch

Color: Blue

Properties when Healed: Communication, Wisdom, Speech, Trust, Creative

Expression, Planning, Spatial, Organization, Caution

Properties when over-active: Talks too much, bad listener

Properties when under-active: Tends not to speak much, introverted, shy

Associated Body Parts: Throat, Vocal System, Mouth, Jaw, Parathyroid, Tongue, Neck, Shoulders, Lymphs (Perspiration), Atlas, Menstrual Cycle

Information Stored Inside Throat Chakra: Self–Knowledge, Truth, Attitudes, Hearing, Taste, Smell

Opening Day of the Throat
Day 73

1. As you inhale, speak the first part of the phrase. 2. As you exhale, speak the second part of the phrase. 3. Repeat each of the twelve incantations ten times.

(Inhale) "My energy" – (Exhale) "is free of blockages

(Inhale) "My root chakra" – (Exhale) "is Centered."

(Inhale) "My Navel Chakra juices" – (Exhale) "are Passionate."

(Inhale) "My solar plexus" – (Exhale) "feels Confident."

(Inhale) "My heart" – (Exhale) "Gives and receives love."

(Inhale) "My throat" – (Exhale) "speaks the truth."

(Inhale) "My third eye" – (Exhale) "Sees past the physical world."

(Inhale) "My Crown Chakra" – (Exhale) "is full of wisdom."

(Inhale) "My chakras" – (Exhale) "are spinning in alignment."

Inhale I am" – (Exhale) "centered and balanced."

Section: 1 - Throat – Element: Opening with Air – Step: Visual - Day 74

To bring in the air element, you will do the visual next to a window or outside in the fresh air.

Put both hands in Throat Mudra Position. This will allow you to send energy into the Throat Chakra. Keep the Throat Stone and Air Stone lying in your hands.

Lay on your back on the floor or ground. Visualize a blue ball of light hovering over you. There is a tube that connects to the ball of light down to your throat.

As you breathe in you are taking in the energy from the ball of light above you, into the tube and straight into your chakra. Breathe in and hold it for 5 seconds. As your holding the light in your throat your throat chakra expands with light.

As you breathe out, the energy shoots straight down your body, though each chakra and out through your tailbone clearing the path of any obstructions along the way and keeping them all aligned with each other.

Breath in again and hold for 5 seconds.

Again the throat expands with power.

Breathe out again and let it shoot straight out of your tailbone aligning and clearing the path of each chakra along the way.

Keep doing this until you have inhaled a total of 10 times – or longer if you feel the need.

Section: 1 - Throat – Element: Opening with Air – Step: Prayer

Day 75

I pray for the air to blow open the door to my Throat Chakra.

Blow away any obstacles that keep me from feeling communicative.

Once this door is open, I will do everything in my power to cleanse, energize, and protect it! I pray for a burst of wind to shoot straight up through any barriers that have been put up around my Throat Chakra.

No more will I feel the need to keep my voice in. I will never speak untruth again. I will see the truth and be able to communicate it to others. I pray to God to feel and hear the rush of the wind blowing through my open Throat Chakra! So that I can be understanding and inspiring and have the strength to keep moving forward on the path that God has laid out for me. Amen

Section: 1 - Throat – Element: Opening with Air – Step: Crystal Healing

Day 76

Lie on your back where you can feel a breeze, and place the Throat Stone on your throat. Rest both hands palms upward on the ground. Hold the Air Stone in the opposite hand to your writing hand.

Remain like this for 5 minute, while the crystals open this chakra

Now use your writing hand to move the Throat Stone down to your navel and up again. Do this 50 times.

Leave the crystal on your throat, and rest your hand back on the floor, palm up, for a few minutes.

When you are ready, take the crystal and rub it in a circle on your throat.

Make 50 circles. Sit up and take the Throat Stone in your writing hand. Put both hands in the Throat Mudra Position.

Both hands should now be in the Throat Mudra Position, with the Throat and Air Stones lying on your fingers. Remain like this for at least 10 minutes, longer if needed.

Section: 1 - Throat– Element: Opening with Air – Step: Ritual

Day 77

Sit somewhere outside away from your home. A park or beach would do well. Place a ring of rock salt around you. Bring a pen, a Throat Stone, an Air Stone, and seven bits of paper (or a large piece of paper that you can cut into seven pieces). Place the Air Stone on the ring of salt directly in front of you.

Sit with your hands in the Throat Mudra Position. Keep the Throat Stone lying in your hands for about five minutes while your Throat Chakra opens up.

Now the following seven lines, one line on each of the seven pieces of paper. (You may hold the Throat Stone in either hand while you write.)

Place the first paper with the written line underneath the Air Crystal on the salt ring, and the others in a clockwise position around the ring. (It's okay if the papers get blown away after you place them around the circle.)

1. *"May the Air burst through"* – Place this line under the Air Stone in front of you.
2. *"And open my Throat Chakra"* – Place this line next in a clockwise direction.
3. *"So I can Cleanse with the water element,"* – Keep going around...
4. *"Energize with the fire element,"*

5. "And Protect it with the earth element."

6. "By using the four elements"

7. "I will be completely aligned."

You may sit with your hands in the Throat Mudra Position again for 5 to 10 minutes, with the Throat Stone lying in your hands. Leave everything but the stones – leave and do not look back.

Section: 2 - Throat – Element: Cleansing with Water – Step: Visual - Day 78

To bring in the water element, you will do the visual in a tub, the ocean, a pool, lake, or anywhere that will allow you to be at least half-submerged in water.

Put both hands in the Throat Mudra Position. This will allow you to send energy into the Throat Chakra. Keep the Throat and the Water Stone lying in your hands.

Sit down in the water and close your eyes. Visualize that the water you are submerged in is a Blue Healing Liquid for your spirit. When you are able to fully see the Healing Liquid in your mind's eye, take a breath in and out. Every time you breathe in, you are soaking up the liquid into your throat chakra. Hold it in for 5 seconds and let the throat chakra soak in the liquid. As you exhale, repeat "HAM"

And let the liquid drain and rinse out completely. Keep repeating the steps until you have rinsed the chakra at least 10 times. Then allow the liquid to completely fill your body from head to toe.

Leave the water when you feel ready, dry off completely, and sit or stand with your hands in the Throat Mudra Position. Take time to visualize the blue liquid you absorbed inside of your body as it drains out of your open chakra. After it has drained out, you see that it has created a ball of light in your throat for the light to turn on, and that the light is spinning.

Section: 2 - Throat – Element: Cleansing with Water – Step: Prayer - Day 79

I Pray to God for His cleansing holy water to pour though my Throat Chakra. Let it cleanse away all feelings of shyness.
I want to bathe in that cleansing water and see all the blackness that has been obstructing my Throat Chakra for so long clear out once and for all. I pray to feel clean and ready to fill the chakra with unlimited artistic energy.
I pray to feel the holy water filling me inside, and washing me inside and out. I

want it to wash away negative energy from my past and leave me feeling STRONGER!

So that I can be open and understanding, and have the strength to keep moving forward on the path that God has laid out for me.

Amen!

Section: 2 - Throat – Element: Cleansing with Water – Step: Crystal Healing

Day 80

Lie on your back with a bowl of rock-salt water close to you.

Place the Throat Stone on your throat. Rest both hands on the ground, palms upward. Hold the Water Stone in the opposite hand to your writing hand. Remain like this for five minutes while the crystals open this chakra

Now use your writing hand to dip the Throat Stone in the water and move it down from your throat to your navel in a wavy line. Allow yourself to feel the drip and wetness of the water on your throat.

Do this 50 times.

Leave the crystal on your throat, and rest your hand back on the floor, palm up, for a few minutes. When you are ready, take the crystal, dip it in the water, and move it in a wavy line from one side of your neck to the other. Do this 50 times.

Sit up and take the Throat Stone in your writing hand. Put both hands in the Throat Mudra Position. Both hands should now be in the Throat Mudra Position, with the Throat and Water Stones lying on your fingers. Remain like this for at least 10 minutes, longer if needed.

Section: 2 - Throat– Element: Cleansing with Water – Step: Ritual - Day 81

Pick a place that has lots of room, where you won't mind spilling a lot of water. Your back yard or a big round tub or a hot tub would work fine. Mix one cup of rock salt with a gallon of water. Put the Water Stone and the Throat Stone in the gallon of salt water and let them soak for three hours. Pour the salt water into six cups or bowls. (Dispose of any remaining water.) Place the six cups around you in a circle. Place the Water Stone in front of you on the circle. Sit with your hands in the Throat Mudra Position. Keep the Throat Stone lying in your hands for about five minutes while your Throat Chakra opens up. Hold the Throat Stone in your right hand you do the following steps.

Repeat the lines below, one by one. While you repeat each line, you will pour a cup of water over your head, starting with the cup in front of you and working clockwise. 1. *"May the Water Element rush through"* – Pour the cup in front of you over your head while you say this line. Then take the next cup, say the next line, and repeat.

2. *"And Cleanse my Throat Chakra"* – Continue in a clockwise direction, pouring a cup as you say each line.

3. *"So I can Energize with the fire Element"*

4. *"And Protect with the Earth element."*

5. *"By using the four elements"*

6. *"I will be completely aligned."*

Remain in the circle for 5 to 10 minutes with your hands in the Throat Mudra Position, and with the Throat Stone lying in your hands.

Section: 3 - Throat– Element: Energizing with Fire – Step: Visual - Day 82

You may do this visual with your hands in the Throat Mudra Position.

Keep the Fire and Throat Stones lying in your hands.

Visualize that every breath is igniting a small Blue flame in your throat.

With each breath, the flame grows bigger until it is a ball of Blue fire in your throat.

The fire is opening your throat and creating a beautiful voice inside.

The fire ball starts to spin, and the energizing feeling increases.

I want you to fill in the blanks below with something in your life that you want to rid yourself of – whether it is a person, a habit, a house, a feeling inside of you, ANYTHING! Inhale, hold in for 5 seconds. Let the fire increase in power. Once you feel like the pressure has built up enough, exhale.

Each time you exhale, visualize the fire striking out a flame in front of you to burn the negative word right up into ashes.

The blue flame goes through your throat and toward the spoken words every time you EXHALE.

(Inhale) "I am communicative" – (Exhale) "I do not want____."

(Inhale) "I am understanding" – (Exhale) "I do not want____."

(Inhale) "I am artistic" – (Exhale) "I do not want____."

(Inhale) "I am able to inspire with words and art" – (Exhale) "I do not want _____."

Now you feel the fire slowing down, until the Throat Chakra is just glowing with a beautiful Blue light.

Repeat:

(Inhale) "My Throat Chakra is energized" – (Exhale) "and it always will be."

Section: 3 - Throat– Element: Energizing with Fire – Step: Prayer - Day 83

I pray to God to feel the fire from the universe fiercely rushing through my Throat Chakra and energizing me.

I pray to feel the heat of the flame raise my vibration to a higher level.

I pray for the fire to energize my feeling of openness. I pray for the fire to burn away anything that is keeping me from being truthful. I pray for the fire to give me an unlimited amount of artistic energy.

I pray for fire so that I can see the truth and communicate it to others. I have nothing to fear, because God has given me the flame of light. I know the truth because of this light, and I can express it because of the heat of the flame. I allow the heat into my body completely, and I openly allow it to burn away feelings of shyness or insecurities. I am open with the Flame of light, and it will energize my mind, body, and soul. I pray for this flame, so that I can be open with the world and have the strength to keep moving forward on the path that God has laid out for me. Amen

Section: 3 - Throat – Element: Energizing with Fire – Step: Crystal Healing

Day 84

Leave the Fire Stone next to a lit blue or white candle for three hours.

Keep the lit candle next to you while you do this Crystal Healing.

Lie on your back and place the Throat Stone on your throat.

Rest both hands on the ground, palms upward. Hold the Fire Stone in the opposite hand to your writing hand.

Remain like this for five minutes while the crystals open this chakra

Now use your writing hand to move the Throat Stone in a big triangle – start at your throat and let the two bottom corners of the triangle be your hips.

Do this 50 times in a clockwise direction.

Leave the crystal on your throat, and rest your hand back on the floor, palm up, for a few minutes.

When you are ready, take the crystal and move it in a small triangle just around your throat. Do this 50 times.

Sit up and take the Throat Stone in your writing hand.

Put both hands in the Throat Mudra Position.

Both hands should now be in the Throat Mudra Position, with the Throat and Fire Stones lying on your fingers.

Remain like this for at least 10 minutes, longer if needed.

<u>Section: 3 - Throat – Element: Energizing with Fire – Step: Ritual - Day 85</u>

Place five blue or white candles around you in a circle.

Place the Fire Stone next to the candle in front of you.

Sit with your hands in the Throat Mudra Position. Keep the Throat Stone lying in your hands for about five minutes, while your Throat Chakra opens up.

Now write out the following five lines, one line on each of five pieces of paper. (You may hold the Throat Stone in either hand while you write.)

After you write the first line, you will burn it in the candle directly in front of you. Then write the next line and burn it in the next candle in a clockwise direction.

(You can keep a bowl or cup of water with you to put the bit of flaming paper in for safety after the words have burned.)

1. *"May the Fire element roar with heat and flame"* – Burn on candle in front of you.

2. *"And Energize my Throat Chakra"* – Burn this line in the next candle.

3. *"So I can protect it with the Earth Element"* – And so on...

4. *"By using the four elements"*

5. "I will be completely aligned."

Sit with your hands in the Throat Position for 5 to 10 minutes with the Throat Stone lying in your hands.

Section: 4 - Throat– Element: Protect and Strengthen with Earth – Step: Visual Day 86

Now you have Opened, Cleansed, and Energized the Throat Chakra. It is now

strong and healthy. It is time to seal and protect it, and make it strong.

Put both hands in the Throat Mudra Position. This will allow you to send energy into the Throat Chakra. Keep the Throat and Air Stones lying in your hands.

Lie on the earth outdoors on your back. Place a rock or a bit of soil on your Throat. Visualize that the energy from the earth on your throat is connecting with the ground beneath you. Straight through your neck in a beam of blue energy. It is securing you to the ground.

With every in- and out-breath the earth's energy connects you to the ground and then moves back up again..

As the earth's energy moves through the Throat Chakra, the chakra is growing into a White Gardenia.

The Flower is slowly blooming with each breath one petal at a time. 16 of the petals are blue, Once the Flower is fully bloomed it starts to spin. The light from the earth on your neck radiates as brightly as possible. It is almost blindingly bright for just a moment. Then its sinks down SLOWLY through your throat and into the ground, while your throat Chakra is still glowing and spinning. Now the energy from your own glowing, spinning chakra gets brighter, and the blue light slowly begins to fill your entire body. Remain like this for at least 10 minutes, longer if needed

<u>Section: 4 - Throat – Element: Protect and Strengthen with Earth – Step: Prayer Day 87</u>

I pray for the Protection of God's earth. Let it strengthen my Throat Chakra so that the lies I once told can never return to me. I want to stand on the earth's ground and be free. I give thanks for the truth it brings into my Throat Chakra. I pray that the ability to communicate with others will always be within me. The earth gives me a beautiful voice, and I pray that it always will. I pray for the earth's inspiration so that I can have the strength I need to move forward on the path that God has laid out for me. Thank you, God, for all You have given me! Amen.

Section: 4 - Throat– Element: Protect and Strengthen with Earth

Step: Crystal Healing - Day 88

Mix in a bowl one cup of soil, a cup of rock salt, and half a cup of water (or enough to make it muddy). Lie on your back, and place the Throat Stone on your throat. Rest both hands palms upward on the ground. Hold the Earth Stone in the opposite hand to your writing hand. Remain like this for 5 minute while the crystals open this chakra

Now use your writing hand to dip the Throat Stone in the soil mix. Make a long, skinny rectangle across your throat, the down across your navel and up again Do this 50 times in a clockwise direction. Leave the crystal on your throat, and rest your hand back down on the floor, palm up, for a few minutes. When you are ready, take the crystal and move it in a small rectangle just around your throat. Do this 50 times. Sit up and take the Throat Stone in your writing hand. Put both hands in the Throat Mudra Position. Both hands should now be in the Throat Mudra Position, with the Throat and

Earth Stones lying on your fingers. Remain like this for at least 10 minutes, longer if needed.

<u>Section: 4 - Throat– Element: Protect and Strengthen with Earth – Step: Ritual</u>

<u>Day 89</u>

Make a mixture of soil and rock salt. Make a circle of the soil-rock salt mixture around you.

Place the Earth Stone on the circle directly in front of you,

Sit with your hands in the Throat Mudra Position. Hold the Throat Stone in your hands while your Throat Chakra opens

for about five minutes. Write the following four lines, one line on each of four pieces of paper. (You can hold the Throat Stone in either hand while writing.)

1. *"May the earth be strong"*
2. *"And protect my Throat Chakra."*
3. *"By using the four elements"*
4. *"I will be completely aligned."*

Now sit with your hands in the Throat Chakra Position for 5 to 10 minutes, with the Throat Stone lying in your hands. Finally, bury the four pieces of paper in the ground outside.

Closing Day of the Throat - Day 90

Repeat the phrases below, following these directions. 1. As you inhale, speak the first part of the phrase. 2. As you exhale, speak the second part of the phrase. 3. Repeat each of the 12 incantations 10 times.

Inhale deeply for 5 seconds. Then exhale slowly for 5 seconds.

(Inhale) "My energy" – (Exhale) "is free of blockages."

(Inhale) "My root chakra" – (Exhale) "is Centered."

(Inhale) "My Navel Chakra juices" – (Exhale) "are Passionate."

(Inhale) "My solar plexus" – (Exhale) "feels Confident."

(Inhale) "My heart" – (Exhale) "Gives and receives love."

(Inhale) "My throat" – (Exhale) "speaks the truth."

(Inhale) "My third eye" – (Exhale) "Sees past the physical world."

(Inhale) "My Crown Chakra" – (Exhale) "is full of wisdom."

(Inhale) "My chakras" – (Exhale) "are spinning in alignment."

(Inhale) "I am" – (Exhale) "centered and balanced."

Chapter six: The Third Eye

Sanskrit Name: Ajna (pronounced "agya")

Chant: Om or Aum

Location: Middle of Brows

Stones: Amethyst, Purple Flourite, Sugalite,

Scent: Lavender, Wild Oat, Queen Anne's

Lace, Madia

Color: Indigo

Properties when Healed: Intuition,

Invention, Psychic Abilities, Self-realization,

Perception, Release, Understanding, Memory, Fearlessness

Properties when over-active: Live in a Fantasy, Hallucinations

Properties when under-active: Not thinking for yourself, rely on authority, rigid thinking, easily confused

Associated Body Parts: Eyes, Nose, Ears, Sinuses, Cerebellum, Pineal Gland, Forebrain, Autonomic Nervous System, Heals Etheric Body/Aura

Information Stored Inside Chakra: seeing clear picture (symbolic or literal), wisdom, intuition, mental facilities, intellect

Opening Day of the Third Eye - Day 91

Repeat the phrases below, following these directions.

1. As you inhale, speak the first part of the phrase. 2. As you exhale, speak the second part of the phrase. 3. Repeat each of the 12 incantations 10 times.

(Inhale) "My energy" – (Exhale) "is free of blockages."

(Inhale) "My root chakra" – (Exhale) "is Centered."

(Inhale) "My Navel Chakra juices" – (Exhale) "are Passionate."

(Inhale) "My solar plexus" – (Exhale) "feels Confident."

(Inhale) "My heart" – (Exhale) "Gives and receives love."

(Inhale) "My throat" – (Exhale) "speaks the truth."

(Inhale) "My third eye" – (Exhale) "Sees past the physical world."

(Inhale) "My Crown Chakra" – (Exhale) "is full of wisdom."

(Inhale) "My chakras" – (Exhale) "are spinning in alignment."

(Inhale) "I am" – (Exhale) "centered and balanced."

Section: 1 - 3rd Eye – Element: Opening with Air – Step: Visual - Day 92

To bring in the air element, do the visual next to a window or outside in the fresh air.

Place both hands in The Third Eye Mudra Position. This will allow you to send energy into the Third Eye Chakra. Hold the Third Eye Stone between your index fingers.

Lay on your back on the floor or ground. Visualize a indigo ball of light hovering over you. There is a tube that connects to the ball of light down to your 3rd eye. (visualize your third eye as a PHYSICAL eye right between your eyebrows) As you breathe in you are taking in the energy from the ball of light above you, into the tube and straight into your chakra.

Breathe in and hold it for 5 seconds. As your holding the light in your head your 3rd eye opens. Just as a real eye would, and it becomes charged and bright with the energy you absorbed. As you breathe out you release the energy through the open eye, and the eye closes again. Breath in again and hold for 5 seconds. Again the 3rd eye opens and charges up.

Release again and the 3rd eye closes. Keep doing this until you have inhaled a total of 10 times – or longer if you feel the need.

Section: 1 - 3rd Eye– Element: Opening with Air – Step: Prayer - Day 93

I pray for the air to blow open the door to my Third Eye Chakra.
Blow away any obstacles that keep me from seeing into the unknown.
Once this door is open, I will do everything in my power cleanse, energize, and protect it! I pray for a burst of wind to shoot straight up through any barriers that have been put up around my Third Eye Chakra.

No more will I feel so easily confused. I will never have to rely on authorities alone. I will think for myself and have good intuition.

I pray to God to feel and hear the rush of the wind blowing through my open Third Eye Chakra! So that I can visualize my future and have the strength to keep moving forward on the path that God has laid out for me.

Amen

Section: 1 - 3rd Eye– Element: Opening with Air – Step: Crystal Healing - Day 94

Lie on your back someplace where you can feel a breeze. Place the Third Eye Stone on your third eye. Rest both hands palms up on the ground, with the Air Stone in the opposite hand to your writing hand.

Remain like this for 5 minute while the crystals open this chakra.

Now use your writing hand to move the Third Eye Stone down to your navel and up again. Do this 50 times.

Leave the crystal on your third eye, and rest your hand back on the floor, palm up, for a few minutes. When you are ready, take the crystal and rub it in a circle on your third eye.

Make 50 circles. Sit up and put both hands in the Third Eye Mudra Position, with the Air Stone held between your two index fingers. Keep the Third Eye Stone in front of you on the floor. Remain like this for at least 10 minutes, longer if needed.

Section: 1 - 3rd Eye – Element: Opening with Air – Step: Ritual - Day 95

Sit somewhere outdoors away from your home. A park or beach will work well. Bring a pen, a Third Eye Stone, an Air Stone, some rock salt, and seven bits of paper, (or a large piece of paper that you can cut into seven pieces). Place a ring of rock salt around you. Place the Air Stone on the ring of salt directly in front of you. Sit with your hands in the Third Eye Mudra Position for 5 minutes while your

Third Eye Chakra opens. (Hold the Third Eye Stone between your index fingers.)

Keep the Third Eye Stone in either hand that's most comfortable while you do the following steps. Write out the following seven lines, one line on each seven pieces of paper. Place the first written line underneath the Air Crystal on the salt ring, and place the others following in a clockwise position around the ring. (It's okay if wind blows the papers away after you place them around the ring.)

1. *"May the Air burst through"* – Place this line under the Air Stone in front of you.

2. *"And open my Third Eye Chakra."* – Place this line next in a clockwise direction.

3. *"So I can Cleanse with the water element"* – Keep going around...

4. *"Energize with the fire element,"*

5. *"And Protect it with the earth element."*

6. *"By using the four elements"*

7. *"I will be completely aligned."*

Now sit with your hands in the Third Eye Chakra position for 5 to 10 minutes, with the Third Eye Stone held between your index fingers. Remain in this position longer if needed. Leave everything but the stones where they are – leave and do not look back.

Section: 2 - 3rd Eye– Element: Cleansing with Water – Step: Visual - Day 96

To bring in the water element, you will do the visual in a tub, the ocean, a pool or lake, or anywhere that will allow you to be at least half-submerged in water. Put both hands in The Third Eye Mudra Position. This will allow you to send energy into the Third Eye Chakra. Hold

The Third Eye Stone in between your two index fingers.

Sit down in the water and close your eyes. Visualize the water you are submerged in as an Indigo Healing Liquid for your spirit. When you are able to fully see the Healing Liquid in your mind's eye, take a breath in and out.

Every time you breathe in, you are soaking up the liquid into your 3rd eye chakra.

Hold it in for 5 seconds and let the 3rd eye chakra soak in the liquid. As you exhale, repeat "AUM"

And let the liquid drain and rinse out completely. Keep repeating the steps until you have rinsed the chakra at least 10 times. Then allow the liquid to completely fill your body from head to toe.

Now leave the water when you feel ready, dry off completely, and sit or stand with your hands in the Third Eye Mudra Position. Take your time to visualize the water that you absorbed as it drains out of a little opening in your third eye – take as long as it takes for all the energy to drain out.

After it has drained out, you see that it has created a ball of light in your forehead and the light is spinning.
Every breath is making the light spin faster.
Keep doing this for 10 minutes, or longer if needed.

Section 2 3rd Eye – Element: Cleansing with Water – Step: Prayer - Day 97

I Pray to God for His cleansing holy water to pour though my Third Eye Chakra. Let it cleanse away all feelings of confusion. I want to bathe in that cleansing water and see all the blackness that has been obstructing my Third Eye Chakra for so long clear out once and for all.

I pray to feel clean and ready to fill the chakra with unlimited healing energy.

I pray to feel the holy water filling me up inside, and washing me inside and out.

I want it to wash away negative energy from my past and leave me feeling STRONGER! So that I can rely on myself, and have the strength to keep moving forward on the path that God has laid out for me.

Amen!

Section: 2 - 3rd Eye– Element: Cleansing with Water – Step: Crystal Healing - Day 98

Lie on your back with a bowl of rock salt water close to you. Place the Third Eye Stone on your third eye. Rest both hands palms up on the ground with the Water Stone in the opposite hand to your writing hand. Remain like this for 5 minute while the crystals open this chakra.

Now use your writing hand to dip the Third Eye Stone in the water and move it down from your third eye to your navel in a wavy line. Allow yourself to feel the drip and wetness of the water on your third eye. Do this 50 times. Leave the crystal on your third eye, and rest your hand back on the floor, palm up, for a few minutes. When you are ready, take the crystal, dip it in the water and move in a wavy line from one temple to the other, crossing the third eye in the middle. Do this 50 times. Sit up and put both hands in the Third Eye Mudra Position, holding the Water Stone between your two index fingers. Keep the Third Eye Stone in front of you on the floor. Remain like this for at least 10 minutes, longer if needed.

<u>Section: 2 - 3rd Eye – Element: Cleansing with Water – Step: Ritual - Day 99</u>

You will need a place that has lots of room, where you won't mind spilling a lot of water. Your back yard or a big round tub or hot tub is fine. Mix one cup of rock salt with a gallon of water. Put the Water Stone and the Third Eye Stone in the gallon of salt water and let it soak for three hours. Pour salt water into six cups or bowls. (Dispose of any water remaining.)

Place the six cups around you in a circle.

Place the Water Stone on the circle in front of you.

Sit with your hands in the Third Eye Mudra Position for 5 minutes (hold the Third Eye Stone between your index fingers), while your Third Eye Chakra opens up.

Hold the Third Eye Stone in your right hand while you do the following steps.

Repeat the next six lines one by one.

While you repeat each line, you will pour one cup of water over your head, starting with the cup in front of you and working clockwise.

1. "May the Water Element rush through" – Pour the cup in front of you over your head while you say this.

2. "And Cleanse my Third Eye Chakra." Keep going around the circle, pouring a cup as you say each line.

3. "So I can Energize with the Fire element"

4. "And Protect with the Earth element."

5. "By using the four elements,"

6. "I will be completely aligned."

Now sit with your hands in the Third Eye Chakra position for 5 to 10 minutes with the Third Eye Stone held between your index fingers. Remain longer if needed.

Section: 3 - 3rd Eye– Element: Energizing with Fire – Step: Visual - Day 100

Put both hands in The Third Eye Mudra Position. This will allow you to send energy into the Third Eye Chakra. Hold The Third Eye Stone between your index fingers.

Visualize that every breath is igniting a little Indigo flame in your third eye.

With each breath, the Indigo flame becomes larger until it is a ball of Indigo fire in your third eye.

This fire is opening your third eye and creating a powerful flow of healing energy.

The fire ball starts to spin, and the energizing feeling increases.

I want you to fill in the blanks below with something in your life that you want to rid yourself of – whether it is a person, a habit, a house, a feeling inside of you, ANYTHING! Inhale, hold in for 5 seconds.

Let the fire increase in power. Once you feel like the pressure has built up enough, exhale.

Every time you exhale, visualize the fire striking out a flame in front of you to burn the negative word right up into ashes. The flame goes through your third eye and up towards the spoken words every time you EXHALE.

(Inhale) "I am intuitive" – (Exhale) "I do not want ____."

(Inhale) "I am a healer" – (Exhale) "I do not want ____."

(Inhale) "I am intelligent" – (Exhale) "I do not want ____."

(Inhale) "I take off my blindfold" – (Exhale) "I do not want ____."

Now you feel the fire slowing down until the Third Eye Chakra is just glowing with a beautiful Indigo light. Repeat:

(Inhale) "My Third Eye Chakra is energized" – (Exhale) "and it always will be."

Section: 3 - 3rd Eye

Element: Energizing with Fire

Step: Prayer - Day 101

I pray to God to feel the fire from the universe fiercely rushing through my Third Eye Chakra and energizing me.
I pray to feel the heat of the flame raising my vibration to a higher level.
I pray for the fire to energize my feeling of intuition. I pray for the fire to burn away anything keeping me from seeing beyond. I pray for the fire to give me an unlimited

amount of healing energy. I pray for fire so that I can see what needs to be done.

I have nothing to fear, because God has given me the Flame of Light. I know where to go because of this light, and I can move forward because of the heat of the flame. I allow the heat into my body completely, and I openly allow it to burn away feelings of confusion. I am open with the Flame of Light, and it will energize my body, mind, and soul. I pray for this flame so that I can heal myself and others, and have the strength to keep moving forward on the path that God has laid out for me. Amen

Section: 3 - 3rd Eye– Element: Energizing with Fire – Step: Crystal Healing
Day 102

Leave the Fire Stone next to a lit indigo or white candle for 3 hours.

Keep the lit candle next to you while you do this Crystal Healing.

Lie on your back and place the Third Eye Stone on your third eye. Rest both hands faced up on the ground with the Fire Stone in the opposite hand to your writing hand.

Remain like this for 5 minute while the crystals open this chakra.

Now use your writing hand to move the Third Eye Stone in a big triangle, starting at your third eye and moving down to the two bottom corners at each of your hips. Do this 50 times in a clockwise direction.

Leave the crystal on your third eye, and rest your hand back on the floor, palm up, for a few minutes. When you are ready, take the crystal and move it in a small triangle just around your third eye. Do this 50 times.

Sit up and put both hands in the Third Eye Mudra Position, with the Fire Stone held between your index fingers.

Keep the Third Eye Stone on the floor in front of you.

Remain like this for at least 10 minutes, longer if needed.

Section: 3 - 3rd Eye – Element: Energizing with Fire – Step: Ritual

Day 103

Place five indigo or white candles around you in a circle. Place the Fire Stone next to the candle in front of you. Sit with your hands in the Third Eye Mudra Position for 5 minutes (hold the Third Eye Stone between your index fingers), while your Third Eye Chakra opens up.

Hold the Third Eye Stone in either hand while you do the following steps.

You will write five lines, one line on each of five pieces of paper.

After you write the first line, you will burn it in the candle directly in front of you. Then write the next line and burn it in the next candle in a clockwise direction.

(You can keep a bowl or cup of water with you to put the bit of flaming paper in when the words have burned.)

1. "May the Fire element roar with heat and flame," – Burn this line in the candle in front of you.

2. *"And Energize my Third Eye Chakra."* – Burn this line in the next candle.

3. *"So I can protect it with the Earth Element."* – And so on...

4. *"By using the four elements,"*

5. *"I will be completely aligned."*

Now sit with your hands in the Third Eye Chakra position for 5 to 10 minutes with the Third Eye Stone held between your index fingers. Sit longer if needed.

Section: 4 - 3rd Eye – Element: Protect and Strengthen with Earth
Step: Visual - Day 104

You have now Opened, Cleansed, and Energized the Third Eye Chakra. It is now strong and healthy. It is time to seal and protect it and make it strong. Put both hands in The Third Eye Mudra Position. This will allow you to send energy into the Third Eye Chakra. Hold the Third Eye Stone between your index fingers.

Lie on the earth outdoors on your back. Place a rock or a bit of soil on your 3rd eye. Visualize that the energy from the earth on your forehead is connecting with the ground beneath you. Straight through your head in a beam of indigo energy. It is securing you to the ground.

With every in- and out-breath the earth's energy connects you to the ground and then moves back up again.. As the earth's energy moves through the 3rd eye Chakra, the chakra is growing into a White Spider Lily. The Flower is slowly blooming with each breath one petal at a time.

2 of the petals are indigo,

Once the Flower is fully bloomed it starts to spin

The light from the earth on your forehead radiates as brightly as possible. It is almost blindingly bright for just a moment. Then its sinks down SLOWLY through your head and into the ground, while your 3rd eye Chakra is still glowing and spinning.

Now the energy from your own glowing, spinning chakra gets brighter, and the indigo light slowly begins to fill your entire body. Remain like this for at least 10 minutes, longer if needed.

Section: 4 - 3rd Eye

Element: Protect and Strengthen with

Earth Step: Prayer - Day 105

I pray for the Protection of God's earth.

Let it strengthen my Third Eye Chakra so

that the blindness I had can never return to

me.

I want to stand on the earth's ground and be

able to see farther then I ever have.

I give thanks for the sight that it brings into

my Third Eye Chakra.

I pray that the ability to heal will always be

within me.

The earth gives me a connection to the other side, and I pray that it always will. I pray for the earth's instinct, so that I can have the strength I need to move forward on the path that God has laid out for me.

Amen.

Section: 4 - 3rd Eye– Element: Protect and Strengthen with Earth
Step: Crystal Healing - Day 106

Mix in a bowl one cup of soil, one cup of rock salt, and half a cup of water (or enough to make it muddy).

Lie on your back, and place the Third Eye Stone on your third eye.

Rest both hands palms up on the ground with the Earth Stone held in the opposite hand to your writing hand. Remain like this for 5 minute while the crystals open this chakra.

Now use your writing hand to dip the Third Eye Stone in the soil mix. Make a long skinny rectangle across your third eye (from temple to temple), then down across your navel, and from hip bone to hip bone and back up again Do this 50 times in a clockwise direction.

Leave the crystal on your third eye, and rest your hand back on the floor, palm up, for a few minutes.

When you are ready, take the crystal and move it in a small rectangle just around your third eye. Do this 50 times.

Sit up and put both hands in the Third Eye Mudra Position, with the Earth Stone held between your index fingers.

Keep the Third Eye Stone on the floor in front of you.

Remain like this for at least 10 minutes, longer if needed.

Section: 4 - 3rd Eye – Element: Protect and Strengthen with Earth
Step: Ritual - Day 107

Make a mixture of soil and rock salt. Surround yourself with it in a circle. Place the Earth Stone on the circle directly in front of you,
Sit with your hands in the Third Eye Mudra Position for 5 minutes (hold the Third Eye Stone between your index fingers), while your Third Eye Chakra opens up.

While you do the following steps, hold the Third Eye Stone in either hand. You'll need four pieces of paper. You will write one line on each piece of paper.

1. *"May the earth be strong"*
2. *"and protect my Third Eye Chakra."*
3. *"By using the four elements,"*
4. *"I will be completely aligned."*

Now sit with your hands in the Third Eye Chakra position for 5 to 10 minutes, with the Third Eye Stone held between your index fingers. Sit longer if needed.

Then bury the four pieces of paper in the ground outside.

Closing Day of the Third Eye - Day 108

You will repeat the phrases below, following these instructions. 1. As you inhale, speak the first part of the phrase. 2. As you exhale, speak the second part of the phrase. 3. Repeat each of the 12 incantations 10 times.

(Inhale) "My energy" – (Exhale) "is free of blockages."

(Inhale) "My root chakra" – (Exhale) "is Centered."

(Inhale) "My Navel Chakra juices" – (Exhale) "are Passionate."

(Inhale) "My solar plexus" – (Exhale) "feels Confident."

(Inhale) "My heart" – (Exhale) "Gives and receives love."

(Inhale) "My throat" – (Exhale) "speaks the truth."

(Inhale) "My third eye" – (Exhale) "Sees past the physical world."

(Inhale) "My Crown Chakra" – (Exhale) "is full of wisdom."

(Inhale) "My chakras" – (Exhale) "are spinning in alignment."

Inhale I am" – (Exhale) "centered and balanced."

Chapter seven: The Crown

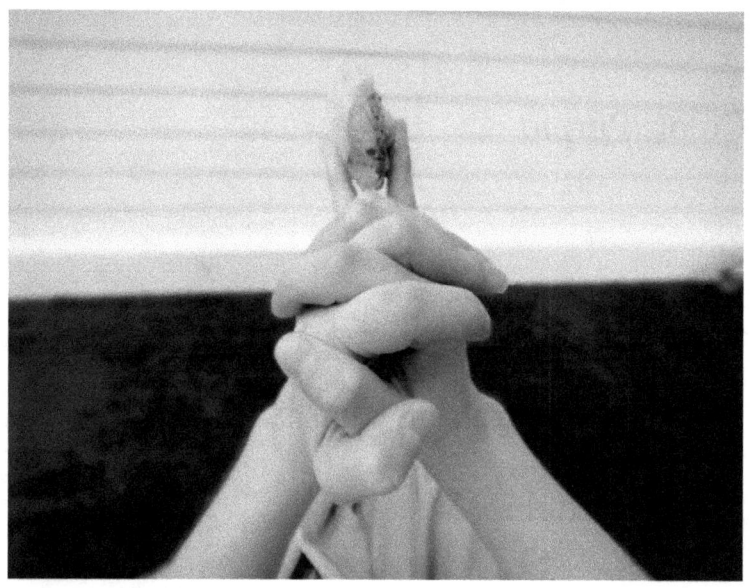

Sanskrit Name: Sahasrara

Chant: NG

Location: Top of Head

Stones: Herkermer, Amber, Moldavite, Diamond

Scent: Lavender, Lotus, Angelica, Star Tulip

Color: Purple

Properties when healed: Knowingness, Wisdom, Inspiration, Charisma, Awareness, Self-Sacrificing, Visionary

Properties when over-active: Intellectualizing things too much, ignoring bodily needs

Properties when under-active: Not aware of spirituality, rigid thinking

Associated Body Parts: Upper Brain, Cerebral Cortex, Cerebrum, Pituitary, Central Nervous System, Hair Growth, Top of Head

Information Stored inside Crown Chakra: Duality, Magnetism, Controlling Patterns, Emotional Feelings (Joy, Anger, Fear)

Opening Day of the crown - Day 109

You will repeat the phrases below, following these directions. 1. As you inhale, speak the first part of the phrase. 2. As you exhale, speak the second part of the phrase. 3. Repeat each of the 12 incantations 10 times.

(Inhale) "My energy" – (Exhale) "is free of blockages."

(Inhale) "My root chakra" – (Exhale) "is Centered."

(Inhale) "My Navel Chakra juices" – (Exhale) "are Passionate."

(Inhale) "My solar plexus" – (Exhale) "feels Confident."

(Inhale) "My heart" – (Exhale) "Gives and receives love."

(Inhale) "My throat" – (Exhale) "speaks the truth."

(Inhale) "My third eye" – (Exhale) "Sees past the physical world."

(Inhale) "My Crown Chakra" – (Exhale) "is full of wisdom."

(Inhale) "My chakras" – (Exhale) "are spinning in alignment."

(Inhale) "I am" – (Exhale) "centered and balanced."

Section: 1 - Crown – Element: Opening with Air – Step: Visual - Day 110

To bring in the air element, you will do the visual next to a window, or outside in the fresh air. Put both hands in the Crown Mudra Position.

This will allow you to send energy into the Crown Chakra. Hold the Crown Stone between your two pinky fingers, and place the Air Stone on the floor in front of you.

Sit up straight. Visualize a purple ball of light hovering over you. There is a tube that connects to the ball of light down to your crown. As you breathe in you are taking in the energy from the ball of light above you, into the tube and straight into your chakra. Breathe in and hold it for 5 seconds.

As your holding the light in your head your crown chakra absorbs that energy and the power of it builds and builds with pressure in your head. When you release the breath, your crown chakra actually shoots out of the top of your head from all the built up pressure and up into the ball of purple light above you.

Breath in again and bring the crown chakra back into your head. Hold for 5 seconds. Again the crown builds with pressure until you release and it bursts out and up into the higher power above you.

Keep doing this until you have inhaled a total of 10 times – or longer if you feel the need.

Section: 1 - Crown – Element: Opening with Air – Step: Prayer - Day 111

I pray for the air to blow open the door to my Crown Chakra.

Blow away any obstacles that keep me from feeling connected to God.

Once this door is open I will do everything in my power to cleanse, energize, and protect it! I pray for a burst of wind to shoot straight up through any barriers that have been put up around my Crown Chakra.

No more will I feel so rigid in my thinking. I will never feel unprotected. I will rely on God's will. I pray to God to feel and hear the rush of wind blowing through my open Crown Chakra!

So that I can be at one with the world and have the strength to keep moving forward on the path that God has laid out for me.

Amen

Section: 1 - Crown– Element: Opening with Air – Step: Crystal Healing - Day 112

Sit down comfortably with your back straight, someplace where you can feel a breeze, and place the Crown Stone on the top of your head.

Rest both hands palms upward in your lap. Hold the Air Stone in the opposite hand to your writing hand.

Remain like this for 5 minute while the crystals open this chakra.

Now use your writing hand to move the Crown Stone down to your navel and up again. Do this 50 times.

Leave the crystal on your crown, and rest your hand back in your lap, palm up, for a few minutes. When you are ready, take the crystal and rub it in a circle on your crown. Make 50 circles. Put both hands in the Crown Mudra Position, with the Air Stone held between your little fingers. Keep the Crown Stone on the floor in front of you. Remain like this for at least 10 minutes, longer if needed.

Section: 1 - Crown– Element: Opening with Air – Step: Ritual - Day 113

Sit somewhere outdoors away from your home. A park or beach will do nicely. Bring a pen, a Crown Stone, an Air Stone, some rock salt, and seven bits of paper (or a large piece of paper that you can cut into seven pieces). Place a ring of rock salt around you.

Place the Air Stone on the ring of salt directly in front of you.

Sit with your hands in the Crown Mudra Position for 5 minutes (hold the Crown

Stone between your little fingers), while your Crown Chakra opens up.

Hold the Crown Stone in either hand while doing the following steps. Write the following seven lines, one on each of seven pieces of paper. Place the first written line under the Air Crystal on the salt ring, and place the others following the first one in a clockwise position around the ring. (It's okay if wind blows papers away after you place them around the circle.)

<u>1. "May the Air burst through"</u> – Place this line under the Air Stone in front of you.

2. *"and open my Crown Chakra"* – Place this line next to the first in a clockwise direction.

3. *"So I can Cleanse with the water element,"* – Keep going around...

4. *"Energize with the fire element,"*

5. *"And Protect with the earth element."*

6. *"By using the four elements,"*

7. *"I will be completely aligned."*

You may sit with your hands in the Crown Mudra Position again for 5 to 10 minutes. Then leave everything but the stones where they are – leave and do not look back.

Section: 2 - Crown– Element: Cleansing with Water – Step: Visual - Day 114

To bring in the water element, you will do the visual in a tub, the ocean, a pool or lake, or anyplace where you can be at least half-submerged in water. Put both hands in the Crown Mudra Position. This will allow you to send energy into the Crown Chakra. Keep the Crown Stone in between your two pinky fingers and the Water Stone on the floor in front of you. (If you are in a ocean you can secure the

stone underneath your foot or leg so the tide dose not take it away)

Sit down in the water and close your eyes and visualize that the water you are submerged in is a Purple Liquid sent from heaven itself for your spirit. It's the most brightest and beautiful thing you have ever felt or seen.

When you are able to fully see the Healing Liquid in your mind's eye take a breath in and out. Every time you breathe in, you are soaking up the liquid into your Crown

Chakra. Hold it in for 5 seconds and let the crown chakra soak in the liquid. As you exhale, repeat "NG"
And let the liquid drain and rinse out completely. Keep repeating the steps until you have rinsed the chakra at least 10 times.

Then allow the liquid to completely fill your body from head to toe. Now leave the water when you feel ready, dry off completely, and sit or stand with your hands in the Crown

Mudra Position and take your time to visualize the water you absorbed draining out of a little opening in your crown for as long as it takes to drain it all out.

After it has drained out you see that Its created a ball of light in your head to turn on and the light is spinning.

Every Breath is making the light spin faster. Keep doing this for 10 minutes. Or longer if needed

Section: 2 - Crown – Element: Cleansing with Water – Step: prayer - Day 115

I Pray to God for his cleansing holy water to pour though my Crown Chakra.

Let it Cleanse away all feelings of being unprotected.

I want to bathe in that cleansing water and see all the blackness that has been obstructing my Crown Chakra for so long clear out once and for all.

I pray to feel clean and ready to fill the chakra with unlimited an amount of wisdom.

I pray to feel the holy water filling me up inside, and washing me inside and out. I want it to wash away negative energy from my past and leave me feeling STRONGER!

So I can rely on God, and have the strength to keep moving forward on the path that God has laid out for me.

Amen!

Section: 2 - Crown

Element: Cleansing with Water

Step: Crystal Healing - Day 116

Sit down comfortably with your back straight with a bowl of rock salt water close to you, and place the Crown Stone on your crown. Put both hands faced upwards. Keep the Water Stone in the opposite hand to your writing hand. Remain like this for 5 minute while the crystals open this chakra

Then use your writing hand to dip the Crown Stone in the water and move it down from your crown to your navel, In a wavy line. Allow yourself to feel the drip and wetness of the water on your crown.

Do this 50 times. Then leave the crystal on your crown, and rest your hand back down on the floor palm up for a few minutes.

When you are ready, take the crystal, dip it in the water and move in a wavy line from one temple to the other, crossing the crown in the middle. Do this 50 times.

Then put both hands in the Crown Mudra Position, with the Water Stone between the two little fingers.

The Crown Stone keep in front of you in the floor Remain like this for at least 10 minutes, longer if needed.

<u>Section: 2 - Crown – Element: Cleansing with Water – Step: Ritual - Day 117</u>

You'll need to pick a place that has a lot of room, and where you would not mind spilling a lot of water. Like in your back yard, or a big round tub, or a hot tub. Mix one cup of rock salt with a gallon of water.

Put the Water Stone and the Crown Stone in the gallon of salt water and let it soak for three hours. Pour salt water into six cups or bowls (Dispose of whatever water you have remaining)

Surround the six cups around you in a circle. Place the Water Stone in the circle in front of you.

Sit with your hands in the Crown Mudra Position for 5 minutes (Crown Stone in between little fingers) while your Crown Chakra opens up.

(Keep Crown Stone in right hand while doing the following steps.)

Repeat the next six lines one by one. While you are repeating each line you are going to pour one cup of water over your head for every line you repeat, starting with the cup in front of you and working clockwise. So Repeat

1–May the Water Element rush through And Pour the first cup in front of you over your head while you say this.

2– And Cleanse my Crown Chakra

Then keep going around with each cup as you say each line.

3–So I can Energize with the fire Element

4–And Protect with the Earth element

5–By using the four elements

6 –I will be completely aligned

Stay in the circle for 5 to 10 minutes with your hands in the Crown Mudra Position.

Section: 3 - Crown– Element: Energizing with Fire – Step: visual - Day 118

Put both hands in the Crown Mudra Position. This will allow you to send energy into the Crown Chakra. Keep the Crown Stone in between your two pinky fingers and the Fire Stone on the floor in front of you.

Visualize that every breath is igniting a little Purple flame in your crown. With each breath, the Purple flame becomes bigger until it is a ball of Purple fire in your crown.

This fire is God's little gift to you. The fire ball starts to spin, and the energizing feeling increases. I want you to fill in the blanks below with something in your life that you want to rid yourself of, whether it is a person, a habit, a house, a feeling inside of you, ANYTHING!

Inhale, hold in for 5 seconds. Let the fire increase in power. Once you feel like the pressure has built up enough, exhale. Every time you exhale, visualize the fire striking out a flame in front of you to burn the negative word right up into ashes.

The flame goes through the top of your head and toward the spoken words every time you EXHALE.

(Inhale) "I am A Child of God" – (Exhale) "I do not want ____."

(Inhale) "I am Protected by God" – (Exhale) "I do not want ____."

(Inhale) "I am Wise" – (Exhale) "I do not want ____."

(Inhale) "I see the miracles of life" –

(Exhale) "I do not want ____." Now you

feel the fire slowing down until the Crown Chakra is just glowing with a beautiful Purple light.

Repeat: *(Inhale) "My Crown Chakra is energized" – (Exhale) "and it always will be."*

Section: 3 - Crown – Element: Energizing with Fire – Step: Prayer - Day 119

I pray to God to feel the fire from the universe fiercely rushing through my Crown Chakra and energizing me.

I pray to feel the heat of the flame raise my vibration to a higher level. I pray for the fire to energize my spirituality. I pray for the fire to burn away anything keeping me from feeling Your presence. I pray for the fire to give me an unlimited amount of wisdom. I pray for fire so that I can know what step to take next. I have nothing to fear, because

God has given me the Flame of Light. I know why I am here on earth, because of this light, and I can accomplish my goals now because of the heat of the flame. I allow the heat into my body completely, and I openly allow it to burn away feelings of confusion. I am open with the Flame of Light, and it will energize my body, mind, and soul.

I pray for this flame so that I can be at one with the world, and have the strength to keep moving forward on the path that God has laid out for me. Amen

Section: 3 - Crown

Element: Energizing with Fire

Step: Crystal Healing - Day 120

Leave the Fire Stone next to a lit purple or white candle for 3 hours. Keep the lit candle next to you while you do this Crystal Healing. Sit down comfortably with your back straight, and place the

Crown Stone on the top of your head. Hold both hands palms upward in your lap. Hold the Fire Stone in the opposite hand to your writing hand. Remain like

this for 5 minute while the crystals open this chakra.

Now use your writing hand to move the Crown Stone in a big triangle, starting at your crown and moving down to the two bottom corners at your hips.
Do this 50 times in a clockwise direction.
Leave the crystal on your crown, and rest your hand back in your lap, palm up, for a few minutes.

When you are ready, take the crystal and move it in a small triangle just around your crown. Do this 50 times. Then put both hands in the Crown Mudra Position, with the

Fire Stone held between your two little fingers. Keep the Crown Stone in front of you on the floor. Remain like this for at least 10 minutes, longer if needed.

<u>Section: 3 - Crown – Element: Energizing with Fire – Step: Ritual - Day 121</u>

Place five purple or white candles around you in a circle.

Place the Fire Stone next to the candle in front of you. Sit with your hands in the Crown Mudra Position for 5 minutes (hold the Crown Stone between your little fingers) while your Crown Chakra opens up.

While do the following steps, hold the Crown Stone in either hand.

You will write down five lines, one line on each of five pieces of paper.

After you write the first line you will burn it in the candle directly in front of you. Then write the next line and burn it in the next candle in a clockwise direction.

(You can keep a bowl or cup of water with you to put the bit of flaming paper in after the words have burned.)

1. *"May the Fire element roar with heat and flame"* – Burn the first line in the candle in front of you.

2. *"And Energize my Crown Chakra"* – Burn this line in the next candle.

3. "So I can protect it with the Earth Element" – And so on...

4. "By using the four elements,"

5. "I will be completely aligned."

Sit with your hands in the Crown Mudra Position for 5 to 10 minutes.

Section: 4 - Crown

Element: Protect and Strengthen with Earth - Step: Visual - Day 122

Now you have Opened, Cleansed, and Energized the Crown Chakra. It is now strong and healthy. It is time to seal and protect it, and make it strong.

Put both hands in the Crown Mudra Position. This will allow you to send energy into the Crown Chakra. Hold the Crown Stone between your two pinky fingers, and place the Earth Stone on the floor in front of you.

Sit down comfortably with your back straight on the ground outside, and place a bit of soil on your crown. Visualize that the energy from the earth on your head is connecting with the ground beneath you. Straight through your body in a beam of purple energy. It is securing you to the ground. With every in- and out-breath the earth's energy connects you to the ground and then moves back up again..

As the earth's energy moves through the crown Chakra, the chakra is growing into a White sun flower with an infinite amount of petals. The Flower is quickly blooming 10 petals at a time. All of the petals are slowly turning Purple, Once the Flower is fully bloomed and purple it starts to spin The light from the earth on your head radiates as brightly as possible. It is almost blindingly bright for just a moment. Then its sinks down

SLOWLY through your head and body and into the ground, while your crown Chakra is still glowing and spinning.

Now the energy from your own glowing, spinning chakra gets brighter, and the purple light slowly begins to fill your entire body. Remain like this for at least 10 minutes, longer if needed

Section: 4 - Crown– Element: Protect and Strengthen with Earth
Step: Prayer - Day 123

I pray for the Protection of God's earth. Let it strengthen my Crown Chakra so that the narrow-mindedness I had can never return to me. I want to stand on the earth's Holy ground. I give thanks for the Wisdom that it brings into my Crown Chakra. I pray that the ability to connect with You will always be within me. The earth gives me a sense of enlightenment, and I pray it always will. I pray for the earth's spirituality so that

I can have the strength I need to move forward on the path that God has laid out for me. Amen

Section: 4 - Crown

Element: Protect and Strengthen with Earth - Step: Crystal Healing - Day 124

Mix in a bowl one cup of soil, one cup of rock salt, and half a cup of water (or just enough to make it muddy). Sit down comfortably with your back straight, and place the Crown Stone on your crown. Rest both hands palms upward in your

lap. Hold the Air Stone in the opposite hand to your writing hand. Remain like this for 5 minute while the crystals open this chakra.

Use your writing hand to dip the Crown Stone in the soil mix. Make a long skinny rectangle across your crown, from one side of your head to the other, the down across your navel and from hip bone to hip bone, and up again. Do this 50 times in a clockwise direction.

Leave the crystal on your crown, and rest your hand back in your lap, palm up, for a few minutes. When you are ready, take the crystal and move it in a small rectangle just around your crown. Do this 50 times. Then put both hands in the Crown Mudra Position, with the Air Stone held between your two little fingers. Keep the Crown Stone in front of you on the floor.

Remain like this for at least 10 minutes, longer if needed.

Section: 4 - Crown

Element: Protect and Strengthen with Earth - Step: Ritual - Day 125

Make a mixture of soil and rock salt. Surround yourself with it in a circle. Place the Earth Stone on the circle directly in front of you. Put your hands in the Crown Mudra Position for 5 minutes (hold the Crown Stone between your little fingers), while your Crown Chakra opens up.

While you do the following steps, hold the Crown Stone in either hand.

You will need four pieces of paper. You will write one line on each piece of paper.

1. *"May the earth be strong"*
2. *"and protect my Crown Chakra."*
3. *"By using the four elements,"*
4. *"I will be completely aligned."*

Now sit with your hands in the Crown Chakra position for 5 to 10 minutes. Then bury the four pieces of paper in the ground outside.

Closing Day of the crown - Day 126

You will repeat the phrases below, following these directions.
1. As you inhale, speak the first part of the phrase. 2. As you exhale, speak the second part of the phrase. 3. Repeat each of the 12 incantations 10 times.

(Inhale) "My energy" – (Exhale) "is free of blockages."

(Inhale) "My root chakra" – (Exhale) "is Centered."

(Inhale) "My Navel Chakra juices" – (Exhale) "are Passionate."

(Inhale) "My solar plexus" – (Exhale) "feels Confident."

(Inhale) "My heart" – (Exhale) "Gives and receives love."

(Inhale) "My throat" – (Exhale) "speaks the truth."

(Inhale) "My third eye" – (Exhale) "Sees past the physical world."

(Inhale) "My Crown Chakra" – (Exhale) "is full of wisdom."

(Inhale) "My chakras" – (Exhale) "are spinning in alignment."

Inhale I am" – (Exhale) "centered and balanced."

ABOUT THE AUTHOR

My name name is Krystal Starr. I was born in Lafayette, Louisiana.

I have been a Psychic and a Healer since birth. (I was taught by a family of healers and psychics)

I am currently located in Los Altos CA. on San Antonio RD. 94022 where I give my Readings, Healing's and sell my Products.

Visit my Website at www.KrystalReadings.com to view all of my services and my healing product line. The Products are specifically made to work with my Chakra Alignments!

www.ingramcontent.com/pod-product-compliance
Lightning Source LLC
Chambersburg PA
CBHW060230190426
43198CB00049B/800